HALFWAY TO REFORM

The World Bank and the Venezuelan Justice System

A Joint Report by
The Lawyers Committee for Human Rights
and
The Venezuelan Program for Human Rights
Education and Action
August 1996

Printed in the United States of America

Lawyers Committee for Human Rights

Since 1978, the Lawyers Committee for Human Rights has worked to promote international human rights and refugee law and legal procedures in the United States and abroad. The Chairman of the Lawyers Committee is Norman Dorsen; Michael Posner is its Executive Director; Stefanie Grant is the Director of Program and Policy; George Black is the Research and Editorial Director; Patricia Armstrong is the Coordinator of the Committee's International Financial Institutions Program and Robert O. Weiner is the Coordinator of the Latin America and Caribbean Program.

Venezuelan Program for Human Rights Education and Action

Established in 1988, the Venezuelan Program for Human Rights Education-Action (*Programa Venezolano de Educación - Acción en Derechos Humanos,* Provea) is an independent, non-governmental organization based in Caracas which seeks to protect and promote fundamental human rights as guaranteed by the Universal Declaration of Human Rights and other national and international human rights laws and legislation. Its General Coordinator is Raúl Cubas; Ligia Bolívar directs its Legal and Judicial Reform Project.

Copies of this report are available from:

Lawyers Committee for Human Rights
330 Seventh Avenue, 10th Floor
New York, NY 10001 USA
tel: (212) 629-6170
fax: (212) 967-0916
e-mail: comm@lchr.org

100 Maryland Avenue, NE
Suite 502
Washington, DC 20002 USA
tel: (202) 547-5692
fax: (202) 543-5999
e-mail: wdc@lchr.org

A Spanish version of this report is available from:

Provea
Apartado Postal 5156
Carmelitas 1010-A
Caracas, Venezuela
tel: (58-2) 862-1011
fax: (58-2) 81-6669
e-mail: provea@conicit.ve

ISBN: 0-934143-86-2

Table of Contents

Preface

Multilateral development banks have recently come to view judicial and legal reform as important to their development missions. The World Bank has become particularly active in this area since 1990, financing both free-standing judicial reform projects and the legal reform components as part of broader economic development and modernization-of-the-state initiatives.

The Venezuela Judicial Infrastructure Project, launched in 1992, is the first World Bank effort devoted solely to judicial reform. Because of the importance of legal systems for the protection of human rights and the recent Bank interest in this area, the Lawyers Committee for Human Rights and the Venezuelan Program for Human Rights Education and Action (*Programa Venezolano de Educación-Acción en Derechos Humanos*: Provea) jointly undertook an examination of the Venezuela project. The study focused on the Bank's judicial reform philosophy and strategy, the way in which the Venezuelan project was designed and has been implemented to date and the degree to which reform objectives are being met. This report presents the findings of that investigation. A slightly different version of this report is available in Spanish from Provea. Comments on an earlier draft of this report from the World Bank's Legal Department are included in an Appendix at the end of this report.

One of the key findings of our review is the need for greater involvement of the non-governmental community in the judicial reform project development process. In particular, national and local non-governmental organizations (NGOs) with practical experience working with national legal systems and institutions have a valuable contribution to make not only to the substance of the reform efforts but also to building a broad-based consensus for reform that is necessary for its success. To encourage greater NGO involvement, in June 1996 the Lawyers Committee and Provea organized a meeting in Caracas called "Judicial Reform in Latin America: The Role of Multilateral Development Banks." Twenty-one human rights and environmental groups from ten countries in Latin America attended the meeting, as did representatives from the World Bank, the Inter-American Development Bank and the

Venezuelan government. A summary of that meeting and a list of the participants are provided in an appendix at the end of this report.

The principal author of the report and meeting summary is Patrick J. Gavigan, a consultant to the Lawyers Committee. Substantial contributions to both documents were also made by Ligia Bolívar from Provea and Patricia Armstrong and Robert O. Weiner from the Lawyers Committee. The report was edited by George Black, the Lawyers Committee's Research and Editorial Director. Elissa Steglich, Leslie Conner, Olga Villasmil and Jaqueline Peñaloza provided important administrative support. Mauricio Claudio coordinated the international arrangements for the meeting and Ligia Bolívar and Ursula Straka organized the meeting in Caracas. German Sarmiento and Claudia Mora of the *Fundación para la Defensa del Interés Público* (Fundepublico) in Colombia also provided valuable organizational assistance in connection with the meeting.

Our review has benefited greatly from the contributions of many others. We appreciated the cooperation we have received from World Bank staff in preparing this report and in connection with the Caracas meeting. In particular, we would like to thank Waleed H. Malik from Country Department 3 of the Latin America and the Caribbean Regional Office and Douglas A. Webb and Roberto G. MacLean from the Legal Reform and Advisory Services Unit of the Bank's Legal Department. In addition, representatives of the Venezuelan government, from the Judicial Council, the Ministry of Justice and the Presidential Commission for the Reform of the State, have also been helpful and made valuable contributions during the Caracas meeting.

While grateful for all of these contributions, responsibility for the facts and opinions stated in the report and meeting summary rests solely with the Lawyers Committee and Provea.

We are grateful to the W. Alton Jones Foundation and the Ford Foundation's Chile office for their support of the June 1996 Caracas meeting. We also thank The Moriah Fund for its ongoing support of the Lawyers Committee's work on international financial institutions issues.

Lawyers Committee for Human Rights
Venezuelan Program for Human Rights Education and Action
August 1996

Executive Summary

Introduction. The last fifteen years have witnessed a dramatic shift from authoritarian to democratic forms of governance in most of Latin America. States attempting to consolidate still-fragile democratic reforms are turning to the judiciary to institutionalize and enforce the new rules for the maintenance of democratic order. Many Latin American judicial systems, however, are institutionally weak, heavily politicized and corroded by corruption, and thus unable, absent significant reforms, to serve as independent and effective guarantors of political and economic rights. Many governments have sought external financial assistance to address these problems. The World Bank has been the most significant non-state actor in the field since the early 1990s, though the U.S. Agency for International Development has made grants and technical assistance in the region since the mid 1980's, and the Inter-American Development Bank began to invest in legal reform in 1994.

This report examines the Bank's first loan dedicated solely to judicial reform, the $60-million Venezuela Judicial Infrastructure Project (supported by a $30-million Bank loan), approved in 1992. The Venezuela project (the Project) has been "marketed" as the Bank's flagship investment in this area, setting the stage for a number of other judicial reform projects in Latin America and elsewhere. It has unfortunately demonstrated — at times, in a particularly dramatic way — the problems inherent in trying to undertake a judicial reform project without broad government, judiciary and civil society commitment and participation. Although the Project is finally underway — it was delayed for two years by political turmoil in Venezuela — the Lawyers Committee and Provea believe that it can still be substantially strengthened with the participation of government and non-government actors interested in reform. Important steps have already been taken in this direction.

The World Bank and Judicial Reform. In its efforts to promote economic development, the World Bank has come to view respect for the rule of law as necessary for the provision of a stable and predictable environment for economic transactions. The absence of a functioning legal framework could, in the Bank's view, "greatly hinder development, discourage and distort trade and investment, raise transaction costs and foster corruption."

While the Bank may assist member states with reform efforts, it has concluded that its charter limits the kinds of reform initiatives it can support. Article IV of the charter directs the Bank and its staff to consider only economic issues in lending decisions and prohibits the Bank from interfering in the political affairs of its members. The Bank's General Counsel has stated that these provisions restrict Bank involvement to projects that are related to the development of a legal framework appropriate to a market economy and that any Bank-financed reform initiative must have "direct and obvious" implications for economic development.

This interpretation of the charter has created tensions in the Bank's approach to reform, particularly in relation to the issues of judicial independence and autonomy. The tension arises when the achievement of the reform goal of a judiciary able to make fair, consistent and transparent decisions runs up against the necessity for constitutional changes in the manner in which judges are selected, governed and removed. This tension was resolved at the beginning of Bank involvement in judicial reform by avoiding the structural (constitutional) issues entirely and focusing instead on reforming the administration of the judicial system. Consistent with the Bank's early view of its role in legal reform, the Venezuela Project was originally designed to focus on administrative and management reforms and the training of judges.

A 1995 Bank report on its early activities in this area reached a number of important conclusions. The review asserted that: i) the role of the reforming state is critical to the success of any judicial program; reform should not be imposed from outside; ii) reform measures benefit from a prior comprehensive diagnostic study that lays the groundwork for a comprehensive strategy; iii) judicial reform should be viewed as a long-term process, with states prioritizing reform measures and phasing them in over time; iv) judicial sector reform should be centrally coordinated from within the country, as reform programs often involve or affect several governmental organizations with diverse and sometimes competing interests; and v) reform should not be a closed operation between the Bank and the justice ministry but should reflect the participation of those individuals and groups in the country particularly affected by reform — the judiciary, bar associations, lawyers, and law professors. The Lawyers Committee and Provea believe that these "lessons" — with a few additions and some important clarifications — are crucial for the success of judicial reform. As noted in the critique of the Bank's role in the Venezuela Project, the Bank's record to date in each of these areas has, unfortunately, been mixed at best.

The Venezuelan Judicial Sector. Although Venezuela's Constitution established an independent judiciary, the role of the courts was marginalized by the efforts of the party-controlled state to provide for the economic, social and cultural development of its citizens. The parties came to dominate all aspects of social and economic life, and led to the heavy politicization of — and corruption in — most state functions, including the judiciary. In the 1980s, the break-down of OPEC and the dramatic fall of international oil prices triggered an economic and political crisis which shook Venezuela's party-dominated political structure to its roots. The austerity measures imposed by President Carlos Andrés Pérez to address the country's economic problems led to daily protests which were often violently repressed by the police. The resulting political unrest, including two coup attempts in 1992, buffeted Pérez and corruption charges finally drove him from office in 1993. After a brief pause during the interim Velázquez administration, the unrest has continued under President Caldera.

In many ways, the judiciary symbolized all that had gone wrong with Venezuela's political system. The roots of the crisis in the judiciary intertwine several areas: political interference, corruption, institutional neglect, and the failure to provide access to justice for the vast part of the Venezuelan population.

The administrative and management problems resulting from years of institutional neglect and the lack of judicial training are areas the Project specifically targets. However, the extraordinary corrosion of the judicial function brought about by extensive political interference and corruption are areas neither the Bank, the Judicial Council, the Congress or the President have yet to address credibly. The most egregious manifestation of the collapse of the judicial sector, beyond the disdain for the courts reflected in the citizenry, has been the wholesale eclipse of the fundamental role of judges in the protection of the human rights of Venezuelan citizens.

Human Rights in Venezuela. The violent repression of social protest in the wake of President Pérez' austerity measures left hundreds dead. By 1992, the list of problems had become lengthy, including persistent arbitrary and excessively lengthy detentions, abuse of detainees, extrajudicial killings by the police and military, the failure to punish police and security officers accused of abuses, corruption and gross inefficiency in the judicial and law enforcement systems, deplorable prison conditions, a lack of respect for the rights of indigenous peoples , and violence and discrimination against women.

The economic and social rights of Venezuelans have also deteriorated significantly during this period, particularly following the launch in 1989 of the World Bank/IMF-assisted structural adjustment program. Several years of high inflation, currency devaluation and diminishing government social spending have contributed to a dramatic rise in poverty and its attendant social and health ills. These conditions served to increase social unrest, as well as the possibility of inappropriate or excessive reaction by the governmental authorities.

Recent Venezuelan presidents have returned to a tradition of suspending constitutional guarantees whenever an economic or political crisis appears. President Carlos Andrés Pérez suspended guarantees after each of the 1992 coup attempts; in June 1994, President Caldera suspended several constitutional guarantees, allegedly to address the *economic* crisis triggered by the collapse of the banking sector. Although purportedly based on an economic need, the government took advantage of the suspension to take aggressive actions far removed from the economic sphere, including numerous raids in poor urban areas of Caracas, and the detention of social activists, popular leaders, and members of leftist parties.

These violations of the human rights of Venezuelan citizens have continued unabated in recent years in large part because those officials responsible have acted with *de facto* impunity and citizens have not had access to a judiciary free of executive and party control.

The Struggle for Reform. Judicial reform had been nominally on the Venezuelan political agenda for a number of years prior to the development of the World Bank Project. In 1984, the Presidential Commission for the Reform of the State (COPRE) was created to develop proposals for the modernization of the Venezuelan state and to draft the legislation and constitutional changes necessary to permit the implementation of the recommendations. In 1990, COPRE set forth detailed recommendations for judicial administrative and code reform, bills subsequently introduced into the Congress were immediately tabled by opposition to judicial reform and the political crisis triggered by President Pérez' economic reforms. The Pérez cabinet and the Judicial Council ended up negotiating an agreement with the Bank to pursue administrative reforms through the Judicial Council, which would not require legislative approval. The Project thus focused on improving the management and operation of the judicial system and the training of judges, gambling that changes in court and case management, if successful, would serve to stimulate broader reforms later. The Bank's Board approved the Project in August 1992. The final step in project approval required the signing of the loan documents by the Bank and the Venezuelan government.

However, the Project stalled in the chaos generated by the economic and political tumult. President Pérez' ouster from office in May 1993 put the Bank in the position of re-presenting the Project to an interim government, some of whom did not support the Project. In addition, Rafael Caldera, elected president in December 1993, was a staunch opponent of Bank involvement in Venezuelan economic policy. Only at the very last moment, on December 31, 1993, did the government authorize execution of the loan documents.

Evaluation of the Bank's Role. Although Venezuela was the Bank's first free-standing judicial reform project, it has since responded to requests for assistance in this area from other governments in Latin America, Eastern Europe and Asia. This role gives the Bank a great degree of influence to affect the shape of reform. The influence derives from the kind of programs it is willing to finance itself and its willingness to insist that a state commit itself to certain reforms as a prerequisite to Bank involvement.

Recent Bank policy statements suggest that judicial reform programs should "address the political, economic and legal causes at the root of an inefficient and inequitable judiciary," recognizing that "if such a holistic approach is not adopted, there will be a minimal probability for success." Basic elements should include "measures with respect to guaranteeing judicial independence."

In evaluating the Bank's performance in Venezuela, several problems surface: i) the Project was not part of a comprehensive reform strategy; ii) the was no broad government commitment to reform; iii) reform strategies failed to address crucial structural impediments to judicial independence; iv) the reform strategies were premised on artificial economic and non-economic distinctions in key areas; v) access to justice concerns were not addressed; and vi) there was no broad-based participation in the design and development of the Project.

Comprehensive Reform. The methodological debate over the proper approach to reform involves two issues. First, should a state develop a comprehensive, long-term plan for reform, based on a diagnostic study of the entire judicial sector, before Bank involvement in discreet reform initiatives? And, second, how should reform be sequenced — should constitutional and legislative measures precede other reforms? The consensus among those with experience with judicial system reform efforts, including the World Bank, is that reform should occur within the context of a comprehensive, long-term strategy.

Comprehensive reform requires that a government — in conjunction with the broad range of actors in civil society — acknowledge the fundamental impediments to the functioning of the rule of law and the source of failure to protect constitutionally guaranteed economic, political, civil, social and cultural rights. A genuine reform effort contemplates the involvement of all judicial system actors in order to secure administrative and procedural coordination, and it logically sequences institutional changes and budgetary resources — and financing from international sources — for each reform phase or project.

Executive Summary

An incremental initiative such as the Venezuela Project often lacks the base of support within the branches of government, political parties and civil society to guarantee the long-run viability of the project's reforms. The Project's improvements, however meritorious, may well be short-lived if the courts remain heavily influenced by political and private economic interests. One of the assumptions underlying an incremental approach to reform is that judicial independence is ultimately a characteristic of the way judges act, that is, of judicial character and culture, not the result of constitutional or legislative norms designed to provide greater institutional distance between the judicial system and political influences. While such an assumption may be reasonable, the reform sequencing implications that follow conflict with broader reform principles, in particular the need for broad government commitment *prior* to the initiation of a reform plan involving the entire judicial system, supported with input from the government, the legal community and relevant representatives of civil society.

The Project ended up adopting (if not developing) a judge-first strategy as early work revealed a need to move beyond judiciary infrastructure improvements and focus on the manner in which judges perform their work. Consequently, neither the Bank nor the Judicial Council desired much exposure for the Project (even within the judiciary) until the development of management reforms and a core of reform judges were well under way. As a result, the Project seems to have survived (barely) the 1992-94 economic and political crises, but with no broad support or consensus on the direction reform should take.

Government Commitment. In order for legal technical assistance to bring about the desired results, recipient governments "need to establish law reform agendas and prioritize areas where legal assistance is most needed." As the Bank concedes, "[u]nless a country is committed to reforming its legal regime . . . legal technical assistance may be a waste of resources."

No such commitment was ever requested of the Venezuelan government. In fact, as noted earlier, the Congress had demonstrated no enthusiasm for legal reform, refusing to address the legislative changes proposed by COPRE between 1987 and 1991. The value of the Pérez administration's commitment to reform evaporated with Pérez' ouster on corruption charges in May 1993. By the middle of 1993, not a single government minister involved in the development of the Project remained in office; entering 1994, therefore, the Bank had almost no official base of support for the Project.

Judicial Independence. The most serious problems of the Venezuelan courts — arbitrariness, corruption, delays — grow out of the lack of institutional independence of the judicial sector. While the Bank fully agrees that judicial independence is the critical issue in most Latin American states, and certainly in Venezuela, none of these elements has yet been addressed in the Venezuela Project.

The Bank's "Economic" Focus. Bank-supported judicial reform initiatives have stressed distinctions between what are deemed economic and non-economic elements of judicial systems. There is a Bank proclivity to work on commercial codes and civil procedures but to avoid penal issues and procedures and judicial entities that may protect constitutional rights generally but are not seen to have "direct" relevance for commerce or investment. Part of this discrete focus grows out of the Bank's concern about remaining within the scope of its charter mandate and part from the assumption that what investors and merchants primarily seek from judicial systems.

The Lawyers Committee and Provea believe such distinctions are artificial. While there is little research documenting the link between the performance of courts and economic development, available evidence suggests that *political predictability* is probably the more important variable in attracting investment. Moreover, the concerns expressed by foreign and domestic investors about the reliability of the judicial system appear to be a subset of a much broader concern about "judicial insecurity" arising from the fear that fundamental civil and political rights — the right to be free from arbitrary arrest and imprisonment, the right to fair pretrial and trial procedures, the right to be free of unconstitutional actions taken by the government — cannot be vindicated by a deeply politicized and corrupt judiciary. Economic issues are also implicated in the ability of many Latin American presidents to rule by decree or through the authority of broad emergency legislation without effective judicial oversight. Whether concerned about human rights, economic reforms or investments, none are secure if an executive can so easily and arbitrarily change a government's course.

Access to Justice. The ability of those with fewer resources to use the courts is a key measurement of the functioning of a judicial system. Access is critical for small business persons attempting to enforce contracts or defend intellectual property as well as individuals attempting to vindicate human rights guarantees. In fact, access to justice is an area that implicates the Bank's "overarching objective" of poverty alleviation. The Venezuela Project does not include an access-to-justice component, even though the courts are out-of-reach for most of the Venezuelan population.

Participation. Although long-criticized for failure to include non-governmental "consumers" in the design and implementation of economic development projects, the Bank has in recent years moved to increase the "participation" of a broader array of "stakeholders" in the projects it funds, recognizing that "[t]here is significant evidence that participation can, in many circumstances, improve the quality, effectiveness and sustainability of projects, and strengthen ownership and commitment of government and stakeholders."

Yet participation was not a recognized Bank policy in 1990, when discussions concerning the Venezuelan project began. Not surprisingly, many major actors in the judicial system — the Ministry of Justice and the Public Prosecutor most prominently — had very little input, and almost no actors in civil society — academia, bar associations, law faculties, NGOs — were contacted. More surprising is that only a handful of judges were consulted and the vast majority knew little of the contents of the Project other than that which they had read in newspapers as late as May 1995.

In spite of the expressed willingness of Bank officials and the Judicial Council to begin to reach out to civil society, the Project is only slowly emerging from the cloak of secrecy which has covered it since its inception.

Coordination of Donor Involvement. Because of its global scope and interdisciplinary expertise, the Bank views itself as well-positioned to act as coordinator of external legal technical assistance in its borrowing member countries. Yet coordination of activities among the various multilateral and bilateral donors is haphazard. Moreover, serious coordination problems exist among the four entities in the Venezuelan government which comprise the judicial sector. The Bank attempted to address this problem at the outset by establishing an inter-agency project advisory committee, but with nothing directly at stake in the Project, interest in the committee diminished and it ceased to function.

The Project on Its Merits. The Project does address a limited number of the difficulties plaguing the court system. Its broadest focus is on the catastrophic state of judicial administration and court and case management. And in proposing to strengthen the ability of the Judicial Council to actually manage and plan for over 1,000 courts, the Project is laced with studies that are to precede the development of new administrative procedures and technology systems. At the planning stages, then, the Bank seems to be taking a prudent approach to administrative restructuring.

The most dramatic change suggested for the courts by the Project is the manner in which individual judges work. Several new pilot courtroom models are to be tested in a number of different regions. The Project may also provide the basis for improved responsiveness from public defenders. And the revival of the judicial school is critical for preparation for the judicial career and continuing education for sitting judges. Finally, the Project provides a basis for follow-on proposals through a series of studies of various issues related to the functioning of the judiciary.

The success of these modest proposals, of course, depends upon factors originally avoided by the Bank and the Judicial Council: the depolitization of the courts and the Judicial Council, the weeding out corruption, and the political commitment to provide the resources for an independent judicial sector during years of economic crisis. Problems continue to plague the Project, now four years after Board approval. The government still has no broad reform strategy, the breadth and depth of its interest in substantive reform is unclear, and Judicial Council and Bank promises to expand participation are only slowly being realized.

Introduction

The last fifteen years have witnessed a dramatic shift from authoritarian to democratic forms of governance in most of Latin America. States attempting to consolidate still-fragile democratic reforms are turning to the judiciary to institutionalize and enforce the new rules for the maintenance of democratic order. Many Latin American judicial systems, however, are institutionally weak, heavily politicized and corroded by corruption, and thus unable to serve as independent and effective guarantors of political and economic rights without significant reform.

Over the last several years, Latin American states have been turning to the World Bank (the Bank) and other international financial sources such as the Inter-American Development Bank (IDB) and the United States Agency for International Development (AID) for assistance with judicial sector reform. The most important of those institutions in terms of financing and technical assistance has been the Bank.

Historically, the Bank directed most of its work to large economic development projects and macroeconomic structural reform assistance for states shifting from government-directed to market economies. More recently, however, the Bank has come to focus on the importance of the broader political "context" of development, particularly the role of the state, in hindering or fostering progress. The establishment and maintenance of an environment where the "rules of the game" are clear and predictable has come to be viewed as a prerequisite for long-term growth. Since an objective, efficient and reliable judicial system is essential to guarantee the fair and uniform application of norms governing economic activity, particularly against arbitrary actions of the state, the Bank has decided to support legal reform efforts in its member countries. The Bank's first loan dedicated solely to judicial reform — the Venezuela Judicial Infrastructure Project — was approved in 1992. The Bank has since become involved in judicial reform initiatives in a number of other states, including Argentina, Bolivia, Ecuador, Peru and the Russian Federation.

The Lawyers Committee for Human Rights has long promoted the rule of law, enforced by an independent, competent judiciary, as the best means of ensuring the protection of individual human rights against governmental abuse. To that end, the Committee has investigated and brought to international attention the failure of legal systems to protect civil and political rights (or to bring to justice those responsible for human rights violations) in countries around the globe. Similarly, the Venezuelan Program for Human Rights Education and Action (*Programa Venezolano de Educación-Acción en Derechos Humanos*: Provea) has monitored and reported upon the role played by the judicial system in promoting and defending respect for human rights in Venezuela since 1989. Both organizations, therefore, welcome Bank support for programs aimed at ensuring that judicial systems are independent and effective and work to guarantee the civil, political, economic, social and cultural rights of all.

At the same time, however, Bank financing of the Venezuelan judicial reform initiative has raised a number of important substantive and procedural concerns. The substantive set of issues relates to the influence of the Bank on the scope of the reform program. Initially, the Bank did not focus on the need for and the state's commitment to comprehensive reform — particularly the need for structural changes designed to free court systems from political control by the executive, the congress or political parties. Instead, the Bank chose to focus on court administration and management, infrastructure improvements and reopening a judicial school. Consequently, the program did not develop within the scope of a long-term reform strategy, nor was an effort made to secure the political support of the judicial, executive and legislative branches of government or organizations of civil society.

On procedural matters, the Bank and the Venezuelan government designed the legal reform project without considering the views of many of the important "consumers" of legal services — individuals, lawyers, non-governmental organizations (NGOs), bar associations, individual judges and regional organizations such as the Inter-American Commission on Human Rights and the Inter-American Court of Human Rights. The Bank's reluctance to follow the spirit of its own policies concerning the value of non-state participation in this area may negatively affect the form and content and the medium- and long-term chances for the success of individual judicial reform projects.[1]

Given these concerns, the Lawyers Committee and Provea launched a study of the Bank's role in the $60 million Venezuela Judicial Infrastructure Project (the Project).[2] The Project was conceived in 1990 and Bank participation formally approved by the Bank's Executive Directors in 1992. The Lawyers Committee and Provea selected the Venezuela Project for three reasons. First, it has been "marketed" as the Bank's flagship investment in this area, setting the stage for a number of other judicial reform projects (and proposed projects) now under development in Latin America (and elsewhere). Second, Venezuela demonstrated — at times, in a particularly dramatic way — the problems inherent in trying to undertake a judicial reform project without broad government, judiciary and civil society commitment and participation. Finally, while the Project is finally underway — it was delayed for two years by political turmoil — the Lawyers Committee and Provea believe that it can still be substantially strengthened with the participation of government and non-government actors interested in reform. Important steps have already been taken in this direction. The Project might also serve as the focus for discussions regarding the profound long-term changes necessary to restore the capacity of the Venezuelan judiciary to function as the constitutional defender of the rule of law.

The report is organized into five sections. It begins with an overview of the role of judicial reform in the Bank's governance-related work in

---

[1]The Bank has recognized that the participation of non-governmental "consumers" (those directly affected) in the design and implementation of economic development projects can improve the quality, effectiveness and sustainability of these projects, and that such involvement by non-governmental actors should be encouraged. *See* World Bank, *The World Bank and Participation* (1994). In the legal reform area, the relevant actors ("stakeholders" in Bank terminology) include local bar associations, legal research institutes, law school faculties, individual lawyers and the public. *See* the discussion on participation below at 111-116.

[2]The Bank loaned Venezuela $30 million of the project cost.

Latin America and a description of the Venezuela Project and other reform efforts financed by the Bank. Chapter II provides a detailed look at the structure of the Venezuelan judicial system and the serious problems crippling its ability to provide anything resembling fair and efficient justice. The third chapter explores one of the most disturbing consequences of the collapse of the judiciary, an explosion of human rights violations since the late 1980s. The fourth chapter details the struggle for judicial reform in Venezuela since 1990 in the midst of simultaneous political and economic crises, and the role of the Bank and the Project in that effort. Finally, the last section sets forth a broad critique of the Bank's role in judicial reform in general and in Venezuela in particular.

A number of methodological points should be kept clear from the outset. First, the Bank's judicial reform portfolio is still relatively new. While the Bank has developed a body of general information on the comparative functioning of judicial systems and reform efforts in various parts of the world (including the United States and Europe) and particular information on states where sector studies or project staff appraisal reports have been completed, the only Bank reform initiative actually underway today is in Venezuela.[3]

Second, our description of Bank policy in this area is our own, and does not necessarily represent the position of any individual or unit within the Bank itself. It is the result of a review of communications from, conversations with and articles published by Bank staff, judicial sector analyses, staff appraisal reports and related bank publications.[4]

---

[3]The implementation stage of a project in Bolivia is just getting under way.

[4]The clearest and most comprehensive overviews are contained in two Bank publications: Legal Department, *The World Bank and Legal Technical Assistance: Initial Lessons* Policy Research Working Paper No. 1414 (World Bank: 1995) [hereinafter *Initial Lessons*] and Maria Dakolias, *The Judicial Sector in Latin America and the Caribbean, Elements of Reform*, Technical Paper No. 319 (World Bank: 1996) [hereinafter *Elements of Reform*].

And while we comment on other Bank projects, our knowledge of those initiatives is based primarily on Bank publications.

And, finally, Bank policy and practice are evolving in this area as the Bank learns from its experiences on the ground. This applies to the Venezuela Project itself, whose scope seems to be broadening as the project unfolds. Thus, the Lawyers Committee and Provea fully recognize that discussion of the proper scope and content of reform measures, as well as the role of NGOs and other "stakeholders" in judicial systems, continues to develop. In that spirit, then, both organizations emphasize that the purpose of this study is not merely to critique the Bank's efforts in Venezuela but rather to seek to ensure that this and future judicial reform efforts are conceived and developed so as to maximize the ability of domestic legal systems to promote and defend the rights of all parties who come before them. It is hoped that this report will make a positive contribution to that effort.

I. The World Bank And Judicial Reform In Latin America

A. Background: The Judiciary in Latin America

Almost all Latin American constitutions have established republican states based on the historical tripartite division of power among executive, legislature and judiciary. Historically, however, the three branches have never been coequal (and were never intended to be). The Latin American executive has extensive formal power, deriving from the presidential roles of chief executive, commander-in-chief and head of state. In addition, most constitutions give the president broad emergency powers to declare a state of emergency, suspend constitutional guarantees and rule by decree. The executive also has usually enjoyed broad political support as the head of the governing political party or as a high officer in the military. The role of the congress has generally been to give advice and consent to presidential acts, to represent the various interests of the nation and to review and modify laws generally in accord with a broad, executive-directed government program. And even in republican constitutions, the military has often been given a higher-order role to protect the nation and defend the constitution, a commission often used to justify military intervention in politics.[5]

The courts have often shared the legislature's *de facto* role as an unequal and only nominally-independent branch, subservient to the political power of the president, political parties and the military. Judicial review of the constitutionality of the laws decreed by the president or passed by the legislature has been largely outside the Latin American tradition. And while courts have been able to control and oversee some government actions, protect some civil liberties and restrict some

---

[5]For background on Latin American legal systems, *see generally* John H. Merryman, et al., eds., *The Civil Law Tradition: Europe, Latin America and East Asia* (Charlottesville, Va.: Michie Co., 1994), at 602-86.

executive authority through devices such as the writ of *amparo* (Mexico, Argentina, Venezuela), popular action (Colombia) and *segurança* (Brazil), many were not able to defend the rule of law during the decades of military dictatorship and authoritarian rule leading up to the democratic transitions of the 1980s.[6]

A number of changes have generated an interest in judicial reform across much of Latin America in the last ten years. First, in the wake of the transitions from authoritarian to democratic governments, victims of human rights abuses under authoritarian rule have demanded that the military and civilian leaders responsible for imprisonment, torture, disappearances and murder be brought to justice. Second, the democratization process itself has brought with it the need for a legal system that can enforce the rules necessary for the stabilization of democratic institutions and practices. Third, most states undergoing the political transition to democracy found themselves simultaneously embracing a sweeping set of economic changes, moving from a state-directed to a liberal free-market model. An efficient market economy requires a clearly defined set of property rights, business "rules of the game" and a neutral entity for resolving commercial disputes.

---

[6]Lawyers Committee reports on human rights abuses in Argentina, Chile, Colombia, Peru, El Salvador, Guatemala, Nicaragua and Haiti during the 1970s and 1980s documented the inability of the courts to hold governments and armed forces accountable for torture, disappearances and extrajudicial killings. *See, for example*, Lawyers Committee for Human Rights, *From the Ashes: A Report on Justice in El Salvador* (1987); *Underwriting Injustice: AID and El Salvador's Judicial Reform Program* (1989); *Paper Laws, Steel Bayonets: Breakdown of the Rule of Law in Haiti* (1990). The Lawyers Committee has been similarly concerned about the rule of law elsewhere in the world. *See* Lawyers Committee for Human Rights, *Malaysia: Assault on the Judiciary* (1989); *Summary Injustice: Military Tribunals in Burma* (1991); *Kuwait: Building the Rule of Law* (1992); *The Justice System of the Islamic Republic of Iran* (1993); and *Human Rights and Legal Reform in the Russian Federation* (1993). Provea has included an analysis of the Venezuelan judicial sector in each of its annual reports since 1989. In addition, it has addressed judicial reform issues in several other documents. *See* Provea, *Suspensión de Garantías y Derechos Humanos* (1992); *Bases para un Consenso Nacional en Derechos Humanos* (1992); and *Participación para una Justicia Democrática* (1995).

Finally, as the state sheds the control and resources once used to resolve social conflicts, governments are looking to the courts to settle economic disputes between private parties as well as conflicts over economic, social, cultural and environmental rights between individuals and the state.

These sweeping transitions have called for a new model of the Latin American state, one in which the political power once centralized in the executive is shared with the legislative and judicial branches. The courts are struggling to obtain the degree of independence from the presidency, congress and political parties necessary to be able to check arbitrary state action.

Years of institutional neglect, however, have left many Latin American judicial systems unable to effectively respond to the new demands. Most of the new democracies have inherited judicial sectors suffering from a range of debilitating problems. The most damaging are those resulting from the historic lack of independence — the politicization of court appointments and political influence on case outcomes, corruption, a lack of transparency and predictability in decisions, eroding public prestige and the consequent decline in the quality of the lawyers interested in serving as judges. Antiquated court administration produces extensive delays and backlogs. And court fees, overburdened public defender programs and cumbersome procedural requirements deny a large part of Latin American populations access to justice.

This analysis is supported by academic and business attempts to measure public attitudes toward the judiciary. The *World Competitiveness Report*, for example, compares the public's confidence in the judicial systems of 35 developed and developing countries. All Latin American countries, with the exception of Chile, rank in the bottom fifteen percent.[7] A North American academic, Edgardo Buscaglia, collected Gallup poll data on perceptions of judicial systems in several Latin American countries. He notes that "[s]urveys conducted in Argentina, Brazil, Ecuador and Peru show that between 55 and 75 percent of the

---

[7] *World Competitiveness Report* (Johns Hopkins University Press: Baltimore, 1994), at 34-36. Venezuela ranked last on this measure.

public sector have a very low opinion of the judicial sector. More specifically, in Argentina, 46 percent of those surveyed perceived the judicial sector as inaccessible. The same occurs in Brazil, Ecuador and Venezuela, where the percentages are 56, 47 and 67 percent, respectively."[8]

International institutional support for judicial reform in Latin America arrived in Central America in the early 1980s in the form of grants and technical assistance from the United States Agency for International Development (AID). The AID programs were intended to strengthen judicial systems in El Salvador and Guatemala which had proved unable to respond to the human rights abuses committed by U.S.-supported Salvadoran and Guatemalan governments in conflicts with domestic insurgents. AID also has been involved in judicial reform efforts in other Latin American countries. These programs are expressly aimed at strengthening the capacity of the judiciary to resolve disputes in a fair, efficient and transparent manner.[9]

---

[8]Edgardo Buscaglia, Jr., "Judicial reform in Latin America: The Obstacles Ahead," 4 *Latin American Affairs* (Fall/Winter 1995), at 9. Analysis of data provided by the supreme courts of several countries reveals similar problems with court delays and case backlogs. For example, the percent change in median delay in Argentina went from 17% in the 1973-82 period to 48% between 1983-93. Backlogs similarly increased over the two periods from 9% to 48%. Corresponding delays in Brazil went from 2% to 39%; in Colombia, from 3% to 28%; in Venezuela, from 3% to 48%. Changes in backlogs went from 9% to 48% in Argentina, 2% to 20% in Brazil, 12% to 29% in Chile, 9% to 28% in Colombia, 7% to 34% in Mexico and 12% to 51% in Venezuela. *Id.*, at 13.

[9]The United Nations is also tangentially involved in judicial reform in Latin America through its *Proyecto de Fortalecimiento del Estado Democrático de Derecho en Guatemala* (Project for Strengthening the Rule of Law in Guatemala), a program to strengthen the Guatemalan judicial sector's capacity to defend human rights in a post-civil war environment.

The Inter-American Development Bank (IDB) began to invest in legal reform projects in Latin America in 1994.[10] The IDB has organized judicial reform into six broad areas: modernization of the law in critical economic and social areas; access to justice (legal aid systems and protection of community rights); alternate systems for resolution of disputes; administration (budgeting, planning, evaluation, institutional strengthening of the administrative entity); human resources (civic education, law education, professional ethics, judicial training, the judicial career); and logistical support. It currently has projects in some state of development or implementation in Argentina (Justice Management Program), Colombia (Support for Modernization of the Judiciary Branch), Costa Rica (Improvements in the Administration of Justice), Dominican Republic (Support to Civil Society for the Modernization of the Judiciary System), Ecuador (Modernization of the Judiciary System), El Salvador (Judiciary Reform), Honduras (Modernization of the Judiciary System), Nicaragua (Modernization of the Judiciary Branch), Paraguay (State Modernization Program) and Peru (Judicial Administration).[11]

However, the most significant non-state actor in the field since the early 1990s has been the World Bank.

B. The World Bank, "Governance" and Legal Reform

1. *The Work of the World Bank*

The World Bank is a group of four multilateral financial institutions, two of which — the International Bank for Reconstruction and

---

[10]The IDB's judicial reform activities fall within its programs for modernization of the state. *See* Inter-American Development Bank, Strategic Planning and Operational Policy Department, *Frame of Reference for Bank Action in Programs for Modernization of the State and Strengthening of Civil Society* (March 11, 1996).

[11]Inter-American Development Bank, Strategic Planning and Operational Policy Document, *Frame of Reference for Bank Action in Programs for Modernization of the State and Strengthening of Civil Society*, Annex 2 (July 6, 1995).

Development (IBRD) and the International Development Association (IDA) — loan or grant development funds directly to developing nations.[12] The IBRD makes long-term (15-20 years) loans to governments on generally conventional terms (except for a five-year grace period before repayment is to begin). The IDA loans funds (called "credits") to the poorest of the developing states at terms that render the financing almost equivalent to a grant (10-year grace period, 35-40 year loan maturities, no interest).

The Bank's modern focus has been on the large group of underdeveloped countries that emerged from colonial rule during the 1950s and 1960s. Traditionally, the Bank funded capital infrastructure projects — roads, railways, ports, electricity systems, telecommunications — as fundamental requisites for economic growth and its hoped-for effects on poverty reduction. In the 1980s, the Bank responded to the acute debt crisis in much of the developing world by providing loans and technical assistance for these states to reorient macro-economic policies from state to market-centered models. The Bank followed with lending and technical assistance programs to these same states to help particular economic and public sectors transition from the public to the private sector.

2. *Governance and Judicial Reform*

The Bank's involvement in judicial reform is relatively recent. Prior to the late 1980s, the judicial sector had played a minor role in the Bank's work in the developing world and only a small role in the technical assistance and structural adjustment loans which formed the assistance

[12]A third institution, the International Finance Corporation, promotes economic development by assisting private sector growth in developing countries. The fourth arm of the World Bank is the Multilateral Investment Guarantee Agency, an organization providing guarantees to private investors against non-commercial risk in its member countries.

packages for states in transition to a market economy.[13] These programs consisted primarily of technical support for training judges and judiciary staff, introducing word processing systems, strengthening legal information systems and establishing specialized commercial courts.[14]

Then, in 1989, a World Bank study reviewing the prospects for long-term growth in Africa concluded that the continent's development problems were inextricably tied to "a crisis of governance."[15] Defining governance as "the exercise of political power to manage a nation's affairs," the report explained that

> because countervailing power has been lacking, state officials in many countries have served their own interests without fear of being called to account. . . . The leadership assumes broad

---

[13]The Bank's General Counsel has confessed that "[t]he importance and relevance of legal and judicial reform is not new, but somehow it took the world a long time to recognize it. It took the failure of governance and development in Africa, the collapse of dictatorships in Latin America, and the great transformations of Central and Eastern Europe to recognize that without a sound legal framework, without an independent and honest judiciary, economic and social development risk collapse." Ibrahim F. I. Shihata, "Legal Framework for Development: The World Bank's Role in Legal and Judicial Reform," in Rowat, Malik and Dakolias, eds., *Judicial Reform in Latin America and the Caribbean: Proceedings of a World Bank Conference* (World Bank: 1995), at 13 [hereinafter *Judicial Reform in Latin America*].

[14]For example, the Bank has helped Bangladesh to establish special commercial courts to facilitate the resolution of claims brought by financial institutions against defaulting borrowers (Bangladesh Financial Sector Adjustment Credit, Credit No. 2152 BD), financed the purchase of law books and computer equipment for the publication of the Tanzania Law Reports (Tanzania Financial and Legal Upgrading Project, Credit No. 2413 TA) and provided technical assistance and funds for the training of judges and court staff, the acquisition of books and equipment and the establishment of a Center for Judicial Studies in Mozambique (Mozambique Capacity Building, Public Sector and Legal Institutions Development Project, Credit No. 2437 MOZ).

[15]World Bank, *Sub-Saharan Africa — From Crisis to Sustainable Growth: A Long-Term Perspective Study* (1989), at 60 [hereinafter *Crisis to Sustainable Growth*].

> discretionary authority and loses its legitimacy. Information is controlled, and voluntary associations are co-opted or disbanded. This environment cannot readily support a dynamic economy. At worst the state becomes coercive and arbitrary. These trends, however, can be resisted . . . . It requires a systematic effort to build a pluralistic institutional structure, a determination to respect the rule of law, and vigorous protection of the freedom of the press and human rights.[16]

The Bank came to view respect for the rule of law as a "critical component for the provision of a stable and predictable environment for economic transactions as well as a substantive necessity to assure that both growth and equity are served."[17] The absence of a functioning legal framework could "greatly hinder development, discourage and distort trade and investment, raise transaction costs and foster corruption."[18] Consequently, if respect for the rule of law required "a legal system where property rights, contractual arrangements and other lawful activities are safeguarded and respected, free from arbitrary governmental action and from pressure by special interest groups or powerful individuals[,]" then "the proper functioning of the judicial system is of immense importance."[19]

Thus, the Bank found it appropriate that "the ongoing structural economic reforms in many developing countries are leading governments to address the reform of the legal system, including the judiciary, as a

---

[16]*Id.*, at 60-61.

[17]Richard J. Moore, *Governance and Development: A Progress Report for the LAC [Latin America and Caribbean] Region* (June 1993) (report prepared as part of the Bank's preparation of a Progress Report on Governance and Development), at 13 [hereinafter *LAC Progress Report*].

[18]World Bank, *Governance — The World Bank's Experience* (1994), at 23 [hereinafter *Governance*].

[19]Ibrahim F. I. Shihata, "Judicial Reform in Developing Countries and the Role of the World Bank" in *Judicial Reform in Latin America, supra* note 13, at 220.

necessary complement to economic reform."[20] The Bank's General Counsel has concluded that the Bank "may favorably respond to a country's request for assistance in the field of legal reform, including judicial reform, if it finds it relevant to the country's economic development and to the success of the Bank's lending strategy for the country."[21]

3. *The Scope of Bank Participation*

Article IV and judicial independence. While the Bank may assist member states with reform efforts, its legal department has concluded that the Bank's charter, particularly Article IV, limits the kinds of reform initiatives it can support. Article IV of the Bank's Articles of Agreement directs the Bank and its staff to consider only economic issues in lending decisions and prohibits the Bank from interfering in the political affairs of its members.[22] The Bank's General Counsel has stated that these provisions restrict Bank involvement to projects related to the development of a legal framework appropriate to a market economy and that any Bank-financed reform initiative must have "direct and obvious" implications for economic development.[23] The Bank's Legal Department has recognized the opaqueness of this standard and has attempted to provide some clarity, noting, for example, that

> [d]espite the fact that it is at times difficult to clearly define the border line between areas that have "direct and obvious" economic results and those lacking such linkage, the Bank has

---

[20] *Id.*

[21] *Id.*, at 226.

[22] *Id.*; *see* Articles of Agreement, Art. IV, Sec. 10.

[23] Memorandum of Vice President and General Counsel, "Issues of 'Governance' in the Borrowing Members - The Extent of Their Relevance Under the Bank's Articles of Agreement" (World Bank, December 21, 1990), at 38.

been reluctant to provide technical assistance in areas such as constitutional or criminal law. Revisions of criminal codes, training of police or judges involved solely in criminal matters, or management of penitentiary institutions may have some relevance to the countries' economic development, but they have traditionally stayed outside the Bank's intervention due to the limitations set out in the Articles. For example, on the basis of confining its lending to the fields falling within its mandate, the Bank declined a request from Argentina for the funding of assistance for the sole purpose of the criminal justice system.[24]

This charter limitation, as interpreted by the Bank's legal department, has created tensions in the Bank's approach to reform, particularly in relation to the issues of judicial independence and autonomy. The tension arises when the achievement of the reform goal of a judiciary able to make fair, consistent and transparent decisions runs up against the necessity for constitutional changes in the manner in which judges are selected, governed and removed. This tension was resolved at the beginning of Bank involvement in judicial reform by avoiding the structural (constitutional) issues entirely and focusing instead on reforming the administration of the judicial system.[25]

The Bank is aware of the importance of institutional issues such as judicial selection to the establishment of fair and transparent judicial systems. In Argentina, for example, a 1992 grant for a diagnostic study of the judicial sector focused on procedural and case management practices, judicial norms, alternative dispute resolution methods and education and training needs for court personnel.[26] An issues paper prepared by Bank staff preceding the award of the grant noted that

---

[24]*Initial Lessons*, *supra* note 4, at 14.

[25]The Venezuela reform initiative is, after all, called the Venezuela Judicial *Infrastructure* Project.

[26]Argentina Judicial Sector Review (IDF Grant No. 28725, December 14, 1992).

"[a]lthough this issue will not be included in the study, it is important to mention that the independence of the judiciary is essential to a complete judicial reform."[27] A Bank consultant later added that even here "the fine line between sensitive issues of national politics and sovereignty are being approached . . . . The [Bank] grant consciously sidesteps the constitutional issue of judicial independence, yet in the conduct of the studies, the issue will arise."[28]

Whatever may have been the Bank's concerns about this issue in the early 1990s, it now appears that, in principle, the charter-mandated exclusion of political factors from the Bank's work does not prevent it from "addressing fundamental issues of judicial reform such as independence of the judiciary."[29] More broadly,

> [t]he Bank's view is that an effectively functioning judicial system is an important influence on the pace of economic reform in developing countries. There is no inconsistency then in the Bank addressing aspects of the judicial system which detract from the efficiency and fairness of the system and therefore from its effectiveness as a means of providing reliable dispute resolution services . . . . Accordingly the Bank can and does consider issues affecting the independence of the judiciary in the design of its judicial reform projects . . . . As the Bank has noted[,] . . . judicial independence is more than simply freedom from political influence in individual cases. It includes structural, organizational and administrative aspects such as a transparent

---

[27]Argentina Judicial Sector Review Issues Paper [undated mimeo], at 5.

[28]*LAC Progress Report*, *supra* note 17, at 16. The author went on to note that "[o]ne means by which the study attempts to involve itself in these highly sensitive issues is by avoidance of analysis of the independence issue and of the Supreme Court, both issues confronted under the USAID program." *Id.*

[29]Letter dated July 11, 1996 from Douglas A. Webb, World Bank Legal Department, to Patricia Armstrong, Lawyers Committee for Human Rights, at 2 (Appendix B to this report).

> and merit-based appointment system, tenure which is either for life or subject to a transparent renewal system, the adoption of a code of judicial ethics to foster peer pressure for the maintenance of high standards of judicial conduct, judicial budget autonomy, and adequate and stable compensation packages for judges. The Bank's judicial reform projects aim to address these types of issues . . . , along with improvements in court management, case flow administration, ADR [alternative dispute resolution], and training for judges and court staff.[30]

The Bank's clarification of its view of this issue is a welcome development, for it addresses one of our principal concerns about most of the reform efforts in which the Bank has participated — the failure to work within a comprehensive plan in which all of the factors affecting judicial autonomy are addressed. While the principle has been articulated, the extent to which it is being applied in practice is not fully clear. Recent reform initiatives suggest that "judicial independence" issues are now raised with governments — the issue was addressed in a 1994 assessment of Ecuador's judicial sector,[31] a 1995 Bank staff appraisal report for a judicial reform project for Bolivia[32] and the 1996 description of a legal reform program for Russia[33] — and the governments

---

[30]*Id.* However, the Bank still appears to consider some (unspecified) matters relating to structural changes beyond its scope. *See Elements of Reform*, *supra* note 4, at 66 n. 290.

[31]World Bank, Ecuador Judicial Sector Assessment, Report No. 12777-EC (August 19, 1994), at 3-4 [hereinafter Ecuador Judicial Sector Assessment].

[32]World Bank, Staff Appraisal Report, Bolivia Judicial Reform Project, Report No. 13052-BO (March 24, 1995), at 4-5 [hereinafter Bolivia Staff Appraisal Report].

[33]World Bank, Technical Annex to the Memorandum of the President, Russian Federation Legal Reform Project, Report No. T-6883-RU (May 21, 1996), at 7 [hereinafter Russia Technical Annex].

of Ecuador and Bolivia instituted a number of substantive reforms to strengthen judicial independence prior to Bank involvement. There is much less evidence of a similar commitment to reform in Russia. These issues are discussed further in Chapter V below.

Human rights and judicial reform. The Bank's views on the relationship between human rights concerns and the Bank's work have been clearly stated:

> Except in situations where the violation of human rights has created conditions hostile to effective implementation of projects or has other adverse economic consequences, or where there are international obligations relevant to the Bank, such as those mandated by binding decisions of the UN Security Council, the World Bank does not take into account the political dimensions of human rights in its lending decisions. The World Bank's Articles of Agreement prohibit the institution from taking political considerations into account, interfering in the political affairs of any country, or being affected by the political form or orientation of a country. Consistent with the Articles, the focus of the Bank's efforts in the area of human rights is on those rights that are economic and social in nature.[34]

---

[34]*Governance, supra* note 18, at 53. Although the Bank states that economic and social rights are addressed generally by its poverty reduction efforts, many observers do not see the Bank's observance of economic and social rights as inevitable. The UN Committee on Economic, Social and Cultural Rights, the body entrusted with monitoring compliance with the International Covenant on Economic, Social and Cultural Rights, has stated: "[D]evelopment co-operation activities do not automatically contribute to the promotion of respect for economic, social and cultural rights. Many activities undertaken in the name of 'development' have subsequently been recognized as ill-conceived and even counter-productive in human rights terms." UN Economic, Social and Cultural Rights Committee, General Comment No. 2, ¶7 (1990) in UN Centre for Human Rights, *Manual on Human Rights Reporting* HR/Pub/91/1, at 76 (United Nations, 1991).

The Lawyers Committee has critiqued this view elsewhere, arguing that a state's capacity for governance is closely related to its willingness to respect human rights.[35] In the context of judicial reform, the Lawyers Committee and Provea recognize that any improvement in the ability of a judicial system to respond to the claims brought before it should help those attempting to vindicate civil, political, social, cultural and environmental — as well as economic and commercial — rights. Improvements in judicial systems will also contribute, as the Bank has recognized, to the achievement of its "over-arching" objective of poverty alleviation.[36] Nevertheless, a Bank tendency to "compartmentalize" its legal reform work, to classify judicial systems into areas that contribute to economic development and those which do not, generates artificial distinctions inapplicable to an institution where civil, commercial, labor, economic and penal matters are integrated into an interrelated whole.

The Lawyers Committee and Provea believe that it is the strengthening of the institutions and procedures which enable citizens and companies to enforce civil, political, economic, social and cultural rights against the state that provides for the security and predictability necessary for social and economic development. Human rights norms and the judiciary institutions charged with assuring their protection (in Venezuela that institution, the Public Prosecutor, is also charged with assuring the constitutional functioning of the courts) are indisputably elements of the legal system meriting attention from the Bank to the extent they play a role in the maintenance of the rule of law.

Indeed, the Bank does recognize that at least some "internationally recognized values provide some important standards for reform." For example,

> there are basic principles of judicial independence as defined by the United Nations as well as the International Bar Association

---

[35]Lawyers Committee for Human Rights, *The World Bank: Governance and Human Rights* (1995).

[36]*See Governance, supra* note 18 and discussion below at 110-111.

> Code of Minimum Standards of Judicial Independence. These principles were developed to enhance the international principles on human rights and cannot be ignored during such reform processes. When there is no "fair and public hearing by an independent and impartial tribunal" there is a violation of these human rights principles. The elements of judicial reform . . . directly seek to attain these principles.[37]

C. The Venezuela Project

In many ways, Venezuela in 1990 seemed an appropriate candidate for the Bank's initial foray into judicial reform. The government of President Carlos Andrés Pérez had launched a politically controversial and economically painful economic restructuring program in 1989 with the assistance of the Bank and the International Monetary Fund (IMF). President Pérez had survived the difficult first year of the transition to a fully open market economy — a year that included bloody riots and constant protests — and the macroeconomic indicators used by the Bank to measure progress had turned positive in 1990. In fact, Venezuela's economy expanded at one of the fastest rates in the world in 1990-91.

Reform of state institutions involved in economic matters was a logical next step. The reputation of Venezuela's judiciary was uniformly poor, and few in the commercial world believed that it could effectively protect private property, defend economic rights against infringement or provide a secure legal environment for foreign investment and market relations. Thus, Bank involvement in this crucial sector would complement Bank and IMF investments in and technical assistance for ongoing economic restructuring initiatives and serve as the "flagship" for Bank assistance in reform projects elsewhere.

Consistent with the Bank's early view of its role in legal reform, the Venezuela project was originally designed to improve the administrative capacity of the Judicial Council, the modernization of courtroom

---

[37] *Elements of Reform*, *supra* note 4, at 70 (footnotes omitted).

management, the reopening of a judicial school the construction, rehabilitation and upgrading of court buildings. However, its scope has been widening as implementation efforts have unfolded on the ground.

The Components of the Original Project. The original $60 million project agreed to by the Bank and the Judicial Council, the agency representing the Venezuelan government on the project, aimed at strengthening the institutional capacity of the Judicial Council to manage the court system and to improve the physical infrastructure of the courts. During project implementation, however, the scope of the project has expanded to incorporate judges into the reform process and establish links with other judicial sector entities interested in participating in the reform process.

The original project had four components: (1) $5.3 million to strengthen the planning, budgeting and management capacity of the Judicial Council, particularly through the implementation of an integrated management information system designed to produce performance indicators;[38] (2) $19.7 million to reorganize and streamline courtroom administrative procedures and automate courtroom management;[39] (3)

---

[38]This component includes: (a) consultancies to develop a human resource development plan for the Council, to introduce program budgeting, to develop the capacity to plan and manage physical infrastructure, to improve capacity to provide technical assistance to and strengthen the management ability of regional courts; and (b) studies to develop courtroom performance indicators, a long-run infrastructure development plan, budgeting and salary norms, assess the private cost of litigation, assess access to justice by the poor, assess the feasibility of improving alternative dispute resolution methods and to identify priority areas in procedural law related to the objectives of the Project. World Bank, Staff Appraisal Report, Venezuela Judicial Infrastructure Project, Report No. 10635-VE (July 15, 1992), at 17 [hereinafter Venezuela Staff Appraisal Report].

[39]Work in this component involves: (a) consultancies to prepare administrative manuals and implementation plans for the new administrative procedures, implement and evaluate the automated pilot courts, implement new court and case management procedures; (b) studies to assess the legal and regulatory framework of the courts and to identify bottlenecks; (c) training of court personnel in revised and automated procedures; (d) supplies and legal material to provide a minimum set of legal reference materials for each court; and

$5.3 million to revitalize the judicial school and develop comprehensive in-service training modules; and (4) $25.4 million to rehabilitate existing and construct new courtroom facilities.

The five-year project was to be divided into two phases split by a comprehensive mid-project review (originally scheduled for December 1994). The first phase is dedicated to technical design, testing and training related to new administrative procedures; the reorganization of court and public defender offices and the implementation of new automated management systems in three locations; the development of detailed plans for reorganizing and automating half of all judicial offices; the provision of basic jurisprudence materials and office equipment for all courtrooms; the training of administrative personnel of the Judicial Council; the design and testing of training curriculum for the Judicial School; courtroom construction and rehabilitation and the implementation of studies of various issues relating to the functioning of the judiciary.[40]

The highlight of the first phase was to be the establishment and evaluation of several different pilot courtroom organization models (for judges and public defenders) which will serve as the basis for eventually selecting the most appropriate model(s) for the Venezuelan judiciary.

The follow-on phase is to extend the new court, case management and automated information management systems to all adequately prepared courtrooms and judicial offices; continue training activities for Judicial Council administrative staff and court personnel; bring the judicial school up to full training capacity; continue courtroom construction and rehabilitation; and complete the first-phase studies and those designed to prepare for a possible follow-on project.[41]

The project is financed by a $30 million Bank loan and a $30 million contribution by the Venezuelan government. The Venezuelan

---

(e) court and office equipment (photocopiers, typewriters, basic word processing computers). *Id.*, at 18.

[40] *Id.*, at 17.

[41] *Id.*

appropriation is for the construction of new courthouses and the rehabilitation and upgrading of existing facilities; much of this work had already been included in Venezuela's long-term capital spending budget, so the state's new capital outlays for the Project are, in fact, minimal. Of the Bank's $30 million commitment, approximately $15.7 million is allocated for the purchase of computer equipment and software packages, $0.8 million for the purchase of legal books and manuals and $1.4 million for the purchase of miscellaneous equipment, furniture and vehicles. An additional $14 million is budgeted for consultants for the design and supervision of the pilot courtrooms ($1.2 million), the design and supervision of studies ($6.5 million) and for technical assistance and training activities ($6.2 million).[42] In terms of the allocation of Project costs by component, 8.8% is dedicated to judicial administration, 32.8% to courtroom administration, 8.8% to judicial training and 42.3% to physical infrastructure. Of the remaining 7.1%, most is allocated to pay the costs of the Project Implementation Unit (4.3%); the rest is for price contingencies.[43]

D. Other Legal Reform Initiatives

Many of the Bank's economic development and technical assistance programs across the world contain legal reform components. These components generally provide technical help with the development of legal or regulatory frameworks for a particular economic or social areas,[44]

---

[42]*Id.*, at 22.

[43]*Id.*, at 19.

[44]For example, the Technical Assistance and Hospital Rehabilitation Project (Loan No. 3427, December 18, 1991) for Chile provides legal and technical assistance for the design of a legal and regulatory framework for Chile's Ministry of Health, a review of the legal and regulatory framework for the operation of Chile's health insurance plans, and the drafting of applicable regulations.

the drafting, revision or implementation of commercial laws,[45] and studies of the legal context for other Bank-supported initiatives, such as privatization and state restructuring.[46] As of January 1995, the Bank supported legal analysis and reform components in some 300 projects in 96 countries.[47]

In addition, the Bank has become involved in various capacities in several independent judicial reform initiatives which have broadly followed the pattern established in Venezuela:

- In 1993, the Bank provided a US$500,000 grant to Argentina for a comprehensive diagnostic study of the organization and functioning of federal and national courts.[48] The grant followed a number of administrative reform measures initiated by the Argentine government in 1991. The Bank-financed study was to provide the basis for a reform program. A Bank loan proposal that grew out of the assessment was indefinitely suspended in 1995, reportedly the result of an economic crisis that struck Argentina in the wake of the collapse of the Mexican peso in early 1995.
- In Bolivia, a judicial reform initiative is just under way.[49] The Bank is providing a US$11 million credit for the improvement of the

---

[45]A component of the Kazakhstan Technical Assistance Project (Loan No. 3642 KZ, October 15, 1993), provides assistance to the National Bank in revising and implementing banking laws and financial instruments legislation.

[46]The Kenya Parastatal Reform and Privatization Project (CR No. 2440 KE, December 28, 1992) provides financing for a comprehensive review of the basic laws of Kenya affecting the development of the private sector and the privatization and restructuring of public enterprises.

[47]*Initial Lessons*, *supra* note 4, at 29-87.

[48]Argentina Judicial Sector Review (IDF Grant No. 28725, December 14, 1992). The diagnosis was to focus on the operation of the courts, training of judicial personnel, procedural codes, alternative dispute resolution methods and legal education of lawyers, judges and the public.

[49]Bolivia Staff Appraisal Report, *supra* note 32.

delivery of civil justice administration services, human resource management, institutional strengthening of the judiciary, assistance with the implementation of recent constitutional reforms on judiciary matters, improving alternative dispute mechanisms, drafting civil code and procedure reforms and institutional strengthening of the Ministry of Justice. The stated objective of the project is to transform the existing bureaucracy into a modern, service-driven organization capable of "resolving disputes expeditiously; issuing decisions based on sound interpretations of legislation, jurisprudence and recognizing principles of equity; and responding to the society's evolving needs for justice administration."[50]

- A diagnostic study of Ecuador's judicial system was completed by the Bank in 1994, again as a prelude to a follow-on reform project.[51] The assessment addressed the structure and functioning of the courts (court administration, the judiciary budget, planning, human resources, information management, infrastructure, the appointment, removal and pay of judges) legal education, the role of the bar association, access to justice, alternative dispute resolution mechanisms and code and procedural reforms. In July 1996, the Bank's Board approved a reform project for Ecuador. The stated objectives of the $11 million loan are to improve the capacity of the judicial system by strengthening the administration of justice. It aims at "increasing efficiency, effectiveness and transparency in the judicial process by improving case administration procedures; improving the infrastructure; expanding the use of alternative dispute resolution mechanisms within the court system; improving the access to justice by the public and women in particular; and improving court reform and research and legal education." [52]

---

[50]*Id.*, at 13.

[51]Ecuador Judicial Sector Assessment, *supra* note 31.

[52]World Bank, Staff Appraisal Report, Ecuador Judicial Reform Project, Report No. 15385-EC (June 24, 1996), at 21 [hereinafter Ecuador Staff Appraisal Report].

- Peru is also the subject of a proposed Bank-financed judicial administration project. The project is to address issues related to the organization of the judiciary, legal education and information, operation of the courts, procedural law reform, alternative dispute resolution methods and the use of justices of the peace. The stated objectives of the project are to (i) improve access to, and the responsiveness of the judiciary; (ii) reduce delays in the administration of justice; (iii) improve the professionalism of lawyers and judges and the quality of human resources, both judicial and administrative, within the judiciary; and (iv) strengthen judicial and extra-judicial institutions for dispute resolution. The Bank asserts that "[t]he achievement of these objectives should provide a substantial basis for assuring the improved independence of the judiciary."[53]
- In June 1996, the Bank's Board approved a US$104 million legal reform project for Russia, supported by a US$58 million Bank loan. The project aims to "improve the performance of the Russian legal system in areas key to the effective functioning of market institutions" and focuses on legal drafting, legal information, legal education and public education, and judicial reform and alternative dispute resolution. The judicial reform component seeks to improve the quality of judicial training, assess impediments to effective court administration and case management, and assist the judiciary in "reaching a broad-based consensus for necessary structural reform of the sector."[54]

---

[53]World Bank Project Information Document, Peru Administration of Justice Project, Project ID PEPA40107 (June 12, 1995).

[54]Russia Technical Annex, *supra* note 33, at 11.

- In addition, the Bank has a number of legal or judicial reform projects under development or in implementation in China,[55] Georgia, Ghana, Indonesia, Kazakhstan, Ukraine, Lebanon[56] and Vietnam.[57]

E. Bank Lessons

In 1994, the Bank's Legal Department conducted a review of the Bank's legal and judicial reform activities in order to identify problem areas and utilize accumulated Bank experience in the field to guide the development of future initiatives.[58] The Bank identified several important themes:

- First, the role of the reforming state is critical to the success of any judicial program — given the fundamental role of the courts in the political fabric of a society, the state should identify the judicial sector's problems and propose and implement solutions. Reform should not be imposed from outside.
- Second, reform measures benefit from a prior comprehensive diagnostic study that lays the groundwork for a comprehensive strategy.
- Third, judicial reform should be viewed as a long-term process, with states prioritizing reform measures and phasing them in over time.
- Fourth, judicial sector reform should be centrally coordinated from within the country, as reform programs often involve or affect several governmental organizations with diverse (and sometimes competing) interests.

---

[55]China Economic Law Reform Project (Cr. No 2654 CHA; November 11, 1994).

[56]Lebanon Legal Assistance and Assistance to the Judiciary (IDF Grant No. 05-28758; November 12, 1993).

[57]Vietnam Legal Reform Project (VIE/91/011; April 1993).

[58]*Initial Lessons, supra* note 4.

- Fifth, reform should not be a closed operation between the Bank and the justice ministry but should reflect the participation of those individuals and groups in the country particularly affected by reform — the judiciary, bar associations, lawyers, and law professors. The involvement of a broad segment of the judicial community is viewed as important to the continuity of reform.
- Finally, the Bank is often ideally suited to coordinate the various externally-supported judicial reform projects which may be underway in a country at any given time.[59]

As this report demonstrates, the Lawyers Committee and Provea believe that these "lessons" — with a few additions and some important clarifications — are crucial for the success of judicial reform. As we note in our critique of the Bank's role in the Venezuela Project, the Bank's record to date in each of these areas has, unfortunately, been mixed at best.[60] The role of the Venezuelan state was problematic from the beginning: the Project was launched without securing broad governmental commitment — reliance on the support of an embattled president and a weak Judicial Council proved to be a huge mistake when a political crisis drove the president from power. No comprehensive diagnostic study was undertaken and no long-run strategy was developed. Outside participation was minimal: the reform effort was conceived, developed and implemented as a "closed operation" between the Bank and the Judicial Council, leaving even the judicial community out of the discussions. No central coordination of reform efforts has yet been established.

While it is too soon to determine whether the Bank's experiences in Venezuela have led to better project design in judicial reform initiatives in Bolivia, Ecuador, Peru and the Russian Federation, we can note that the Bank has moved very slowly to open up the design and development of projects to the participation of a broad range of judiciary and civil

---

[59] *Id.*, at 11-26.

[60] *See* discussion in Chapter V, Evaluation of the Bank's Role.

society organizations. We also remain unconvinced that the Bank is heeding its own advice regarding the need for broad state ownership and commitment, comprehensive studies and long-range plans, when the Bank appears to be pursuing short-run programs in political environments marked by political instability and serious human rights concerns in Peru, the Russian Federation and China.

II. The Venezuelan Judicial Sector

A. Historical Background

Venezuela's judiciary played a marginal role in the social and political life of the country for the first sixty years of this century. The governments of South America's longest-enduring dictator, Juan Vicente Gómez (1908-1935), and his military successors (1935-45) offered little fertile ground for the rise of independent courts. A brief military-civilian democratic interlude (1945-48) was crushed by the country's last dictator, General Marcos Pérez Jiménez (1948-58). A movement of mass resistance drove Pérez Jiménez into exile in 1958. The newly-legalized political parties met soon thereafter to establish the ground rules for Venezuela's first democratic government.

The political model established by the major political parties aimed at avoiding a destructive conflict among contending ideological groups. The founders feared that political conflict among communists, socialists and conservatives might have tempted the military to step in to restore order or leftist groups to splinter off and establish guerrilla movements. The parties, therefore, sought to give all factions a stake in the survival of the government. They agreed to share political power to some degree, regardless of which party won the elections.[61] Stability would be maintained "by the production of agreements based on a concurrent majority that would ensure the vital interests of the main political forces."[62]

Venezuela elected its first president in 1958. The new Constitution — establishing a tripartite government, with separate and independent executive, legislative and judicial branches — came into force in 1961.

---

[61]For a description of the issues surrounding the founding of Venezuela's democracy, *see* Miriam Kornblith, "The Politics of Constitution-making: Constitutions and Democracy in Venezuela," 23 *Journal of Latin American Studies* (February 1991), at 61-89.

[62]Richard Hillman, *Democracy for the Privileged: Crisis and Transition in Venezuela* (Boulder CO: Lynne Rienner, 1994), at 39.

The Constitution gave the state the obligation to provide for the economic, social and cultural development of its citizens. Fueled by an oil wealth which led others to refer to it as "Saudi Venezuela," the state itself directed economic development (owning almost all natural resources) and provided a wide range of social benefits (free education and health care, subsidized food, gasoline, loans). Using the vast resources of the state, government ministries came to regulate all serious social and economic conflict, using the wealth of the state to satisfy opposing claims. With the government resolving serious political and social disputes, the courts were left without a significant institutional role.

The "state," however, came to mean the dominant political parties. The *partidocracia* (a democracy governed by "pacts" among the parties) created in 1958 gave the parties the dominant institutional role in Venezuelan political, social and economic life. Until December 1992, Venezuelan citizens voted only for party slates — the only individual candidates to face the voters were the presidential nominees of the parties.[63] The parties, in turn, organized themselves into tight hierarchies, concentrating power in the hands of a small number of party leaders. These few individuals came to "exercise total control over nominations, arranged supervision of the electoral process among themselves . . . , managed voting in Congress (through strict party discipline and 'faction' voting) and in general kept a hand in the routine affairs of most organized social groups of any size . . . ."[64] Eventually, the parties came to dominate all aspects of the state and civil society, including the labor unions, professional associations, universities and neighborhood associations.

---

[63]The December 1992 elections were for local offices (mayor and city council) only. The first national election in which voters could select individual candidates took place in December 1993. The open voting policy was not universal, however; the voting law permits the political parties to select 50% of the members of the Congress.

[64]Brian F. Crisp, Daniel H. Levine and Juan Carlos Rey, "The Legitimacy Problem" in Jennifer McCoy *et al.*, eds., *Venezuelan Democracy Under Stress* (New Brunswick: Transaction Publishers, 1995), at 149.

The parties attempted to gain influence in all areas of the national and state governments — including the judiciary. The largest parties negotiated among themselves to divide appointments to the Supreme Court, the Judicial Council and the lower courts roughly in proportion to each party's share of Congress.

The Collapse of Venezuela's Political Model. In the 1980s, the breakdown of OPEC (of which Venezuela was a founding member) and the dramatic fall of international oil prices triggered an economic and political crisis which shook Venezuela's party-dominated political structure to its roots. The decline in oil revenue had squeezed the highly-indebted state to the brink of bankruptcy in 1989, leading the recently-elected president Carlos Andrés Pérez to seek the assistance of the Bank and the IMF.

The crisis exploded shortly after Pérez' February 1989 inauguration. The austerity measures he imposed to address the economic emergency cut government services and subsidies. A rapid rise in the prices of most consumer items began to alleviate the growing shortages of basic foods and goods, but fueled inflation. All of the measures were announced just after Pérez' sumptuous inauguration, dubbed by many "the coronation." An increase in fares for the buses on which the working class depends for transport seemed to spark the chaos and looting that broke out two weeks after Pérez took office. The disturbances were violently repressed by the army, leaving several hundred dead.[65]

Pérez proceeded to negotiate a series of structural adjustment loans with the IMF and the Bank and, with the assistance of the IMF, launched a program to restructure the Venezuelan economy. While the tariff reductions, lifting of foreign investment restrictions, reduction of government social spending and subsidies for basic foods and goods and currency devaluation spurred foreign investment (primarily in the Caracas Stock Exchange), the middle class and poor were hit hard with price rises, inflation and the reduction in health and social services. Daily protests

[65]Given the efforts of the security forces to cover-up the killings, the exact number may never be known. For an account of the riots and the efforts to establish responsibility for the killings, *see* Provea, *1989 Annual Report*; Human Rights Watch/Americas, *Human Rights in Venezuela* (1993).

continued — and were often violently repressed by the police. The resulting political unrest led to a military coup attempt in February 1992 and a bloodier military-civilian uprising in November 1992. Pérez survived both attacks but was driven from office in May 1993 when the Supreme Court found enough evidence to try him on corruption charges. Ramón J. Velázquez, a highly-regarded historian and senator, was elected Interim President by the Congress, and served out the last eight months of the Pérez term. Rafael Caldera, the founder of Venezuela's Christian Democratic party, COPEI, and a former president (1968-73), led a coalition of smaller parties to a slender victory in the December 1993 election, winning the presidency with 30% of the vote.

Caldera's victory brought only a brief pause to the crisis. As he assumed office in February 1994, the Venezuelan banking system collapsed under a cloud of mismanagement, theft and fraud. As most of the banking sector's owners and managers fled the country, Caldera launched a bail-out of the sector, investing an amount equal to sixteen percent of the state's annual gross domestic product in a period of a few months. The influx of huge sums set off inflation, a run on the Venezuelan currency and the flight of dollars out of the country, leading Caldera to impose price and currency controls in March. The Caldera government struggled unsuccessfully to develop and implement an economic plan over the next two years, while inflation rose to 65% in 1994 and 60% in 1995. The Venezuelan currency, the Bolivar, continued to slide in controlled "mini-devaluations," dropping from Bs 170/US$ at the end of 1994 to Bs 290/US$ at the end of 1995. In April 1996, Caldera ended two years of efforts to control the Bolivar and removed all currency controls. The currency immediately slipped to Bs 500/US$, and stabilized to Bs 470-480/US$ as of May 1996.

Political Crisis and the Judiciary. In many ways, the judiciary symbolized all that had gone wrong with Venezuela's political system. Rather than serving the constitutional role of defender of the rule of law and protector of the human rights of Venezuelan citizens against the government, the courts had often become highly politicized adjuncts of the parties. They were manipulated by groups of lawyers, judges, political and business actors for private economic gain. And court procedures had become so slow, cumbersome and unreliable that disputants avoided them at all costs. The roots of the crisis in the judiciary intertwine several areas: political interference, corruption, institutional neglect, and the failure to provide access to justice for the vast part of the Venezuelan population. These problems reflect the vast differences between the national role for the judiciary established by the Constitution and the part it has come to play today.

B. Constitutional Structure of the Judiciary

Laying the institutional foundations for a democratic republic, the 1961 Constitution subjects the government to the rule of law[66] enforced by an independent judiciary.[67] The judicial sector is comprised of three constitutionally-established entities (each with its own set of administrative and functional responsibilities), the Supreme Court (*Corte Suprema de Justicia*), the Public Ministry (*Ministerio Publico*) and the Judicial Council (*Consejo de la Judicatura*), and one executive agency, the Ministry of Justice (*Ministerio de Justicia*).

The Supreme Court has the power to determine the constitutionality of all laws, administrative regulations, executive decrees and legislative and executive acts.[68] It governed the judicial system until 1970, when management responsibility for all courts below the Supreme Court was

[66]Article 117 of the Venezuelan Constitution states that "the Constitution and the laws define the powers of the government, to which norms the government must subject itself."

[67]Article 118 establishes the traditional separation of powers; Article 205 establishes the autonomy and independence of judges; and Article 207 mandates the creation of a legal regime to assure judicial independence, including the administrative establishment of the judicial career. Article I of the implementing legislation for the judiciary, the *Ley Orgánica del Poder Judicial* (Organic Law of the Judicial Power), reaffirms that "the Judicial Power is independent of the other branches of government in the exercise of its functions."

[68]Constitution of the Republic of Venezuela, Articles 211 and 215.

transferred to the Judicial Council. The court is now has administrative responsibility only for its own affairs.

The Public Ministry, headed by the Public Prosecutor (*Fiscal General*), has a broad constitutional mandate to guarantee that the constitution and laws of the Republic, including human rights, are fully observed.[69] The Prosecutor's broad mandate includes ensuring the constitutional functioning of the courts.[70] The Public Prosecutor can investigate any alleged violation of the Constitution and laws and may to request a prosecuting judge to open a civil or criminal case where appropriate.

The Judicial Council administers the system of 1,110 municipal, penal, criminal and appellate non-military courts below the Supreme Court. The Council is comprised of five judges, three designated by the Supreme Court, one by the Congress and one by the President. The Council appoints, trains, monitors, evaluates and disciplines judges. It prepares and negotiates an annual budget for the courts with the executive budget office. It has the administrative autonomy to undertake measures to improve the administrative functioning of the court system. The Bank Project is administered by the Judicial Council.

The Ministry of Justice manages the nation's prisons and a national police force, the Judicial Technical Police (*Policia Técnica Judicial*), which serves as the investigative arm of the judicial sector. The PTJ, as it is commonly known, is responsible for formally filing the complaint which initiates a criminal proceeding and for collecting the evidence to be used in a criminal trial.

Finally, the Venezuelan armed forces has its own system of military courts. Under the 1938 Military Code of Justice, military courts have jurisdiction over members of the armed forces who violate the military

---

[69] *Id.*, Articles 218 and 220.

[70] The Constitution calls upon the Public Prosecutor to defend the independence and autonomy of judges in the exercise of their functions; to assure strict compliance with constitutional standards in criminal cases, including the right of each defendant to counsel; to defend the rights of prisoners; to file writs of *habeas corpus* in cases of unlawful detention; and to initiate criminal action whenever the Public Prosecutor believes a crime has been committed.

code (or who commit common crimes while on active duty) and over civilians charged with crimes under the military code. The reach of the military courts into the arena of civilian justice — particularly when members of the armed forces are accused of human rights abuses — is a concern addressed below.[71]

C. The Role of the Judge

Venezuela's civil law model places the management and development of civil and criminal cases in the hands of the judge, who plays the role of prosecutor, grand jury and determiner of both fact and law in a given matter. The parties to a case — and their lawyers — have relatively little control and remain at a distance from the proceedings. Precedent is generally not an important jurisprudential value as each judge theoretically has the obligation to interpret the code as he or she understands it. The absence of precedent as a constraint increases the discretion of judges by permitting various interpretations of the same code provisions. It places great importance on the supervisory role of appellate courts, particularly the Supreme Court, to constrain undue discretion and its possibilities for abuse. Legal norms tend to be applied in a very formal manner where the ability to literally comply with procedural requirements may be more important than the normative issue at stake. Finally, court processes are almost entirely written, requiring significant amounts of time for even the simplest of proceedings.

The Venezuelan judgeship is an administrative career, governed by the Judicial Career Law *(Ley de Carrera Judicial),* with a maximum duration of thirty-five years before mandatory retirement.[72] A judicial career generally covers four progressively higher court appointments: municipal or parish; district or department; trial courts of first instance; and the superior (appellate) courts. Normally, a new judge enters the judicial career at the municipal or parish level and progressively moves up to

---

[71]*See* below at 54-55.

[72]Judicial Career Law, Articles 7 and 8.

higher courts, spending at least five years in one level before being eligible to ascend.[73]

Selection. The magistrates of the Supreme Court are elected by the two chambers of Congress, the Senate and the House of Deputies, for periods of nine years in staggered sets of three-year terms.[74] The Congress also designates one member of the Judicial Council; the Supreme Court appoints three members and the President, one.[75] In contrast to the staggered terms of the Supreme Court, all five Council members are appointed at the same time and serve the same five-year period. The term begins in conjunction with the five-year mandate of the newly-elected president and Congress, giving each new administration the opportunity to shape its own Judicial Council.

Since the Judicial Career Law came into force in 1981, the selection of all judges is theoretically merit-based, determined by competitive written and oral examinations open to the public.[76] In the case where a number of judges have similar qualifications for appointment to a higher court, the Judicial Council may select a judge based upon a competitive review of the written qualifications of each candidate.[77] Judicial candidates who have successfully completed the examination (or qualifications review for appointment to a higher court) become "titled" judges (*jueces titulares*) for the court to which they are assigned. However, the Judicial Council has the authority to appoint "temporary" or "interim" judges (*jueces provisorios*) without examination to vacant courts until an appointment can be made as a result of a competitive exam.[78]

---

[73]*Id.*, Articles 12 and 30.

[74]Venezuelan Constitution, Article 214; Organic Law of the Supreme Court of Justice, Article 4.

[75]Organic Law of the Judicial Council, Article 8.

[76]*Id.*, Article 27.

[77]*Id.*, Article 21.

[78]*Id.*, Article 28.

This exceptional appointment power, however, has long been the norm in the selection of Venezuelan judges.

During 1994, the Judicial Council filled 11 of 16 vacancies through competitive examination; 8 of 15 court vacancies were filled by promotion of lower court judges; and 55 vacancies were filled via "temporary" appointments without examination.[79] Although almost 550 judges have been appointed through the processes contemplated by the Judicial Career Law (open competition, promotion) in the last five years, fully two-thirds of the sitting magistrates were selected via other criteria, principally appointments as "provisional" judges.[80]

Training. A Judicial School under the administration of the Judicial Council was established in 1982 in order to provide the courses in jurisprudence and practical training necessary for judicial candidates to succeed in the competitive exams and to establish ongoing educational programs for sitting judges. The Judicial Council administers the school and is responsible for the content of its courses and programs.[81] Basic theory and practice courses are required of all candidates entering the judicial career.[82] However, the School was never given the staff or financial resources to enable it to offer an extensive, career-long set of training classes. Its initial program consisted of a truncated eight-month course for lawyers interested in entering the judicial career with no follow-up or continuing education opportunities.[83] But its work went unutilized since judges were often effectively selected by the political parties; few of its graduates actually became judges. Consequently, the School closed in the mid-1980s. It reopened in 1990 on a limited basis, offering short-term classes to prepare candidates for the competitive exams for judicial selection which began in 1992. The School offered no

---

[79]Judicial Council, *Memoria y Cuenta 1994*, at 6.

[80]Provea, *1995 Annual Report*, at 84.

[81]Judicial Career Law, Article 68.

[82]*Id.*, Article 14.

[83]Interview with director of the Judicial School, Caracas, May 1995.

programs for sitting judges, despite the fact that most have no formal judicial training.

Supervision and Discipline. The Judicial Council bears the responsibility of supervising the administrative functioning and individual performance of all judges (except for the members of the Supreme Court and the Council itself, who are essentially self-policing, subject to political control via the appointment process).[84] Individual courts are subject to annual inspection and each judge must render ongoing administrative accounts (caseload composition and status, *etc.*) to the Council. Similarly, the Council is responsible for instituting and deciding disciplinary proceedings against judges and public defenders accused of ethical or procedural violations.[85] The Supreme Court and the superior courts may levy fines against judges of the lower court and the Judicial Council may admonish, suspend, remove or bring civil or criminal complaints against judges, depending upon the seriousness of the offense.[86] In addition, disciplinary proceedings may be initiated by sworn complaint by any aggrieved party or the Public Ministry. This procedure remains secret until the Council decides the merits of the complaint.[87]

D. Political Interference: Parties, President and Military

The Political Parties. Although the 1961 Constitution provided for the establishment of independent courts, the two dominant political parties to emerge in the new democracy, Democratic Action (*Acción Democrática*:

---

[84]Organic Law of the Judicial Council, Article 28.

[85]Procedurally, the Council sits as a Disciplinary Tribunal (*Tribunal Disciplinario*) and designates a member to review a complaint against a judge and to prepare a report for the full Council. Organic Law of the Judicial Council, Article 43.

[86]*Id.*, Articles 42-44.

[87]*Id.*, Articles 53-55. The fact that the Council has the authority to levy a heavy fine against parties bringing claims it deems unsubstantiated may serve to deter valid claims as well.

AD), a social democratic party, and COPEI, sought to include the judicial sector in their clientist policies at the outset of the democratic era. To do so, they postponed the formation of the Judicial Council — the entity contemplated by the Constitution to independently administer the lower courts — until 1969, maintaining political control over judicial appointments through the Ministry of Justice.[88] The Judicial Council itself was the outgrowth of a heated conflict between COPEI and AD after COPEI leader Rafael Caldera won the presidency 1968 (AD candidates had won the prior two elections) and AD pushed for the Council's creation to protect judges affiliated with the party. Despite President Caldera's veto, the AD-dominated Congress approved the creation of the Council in 1969. Party control, however, simply shifted from specific judicial appointments to the Judicial Council itself.[89]

The members of the Judicial Council, in turn, faced pressure from their respective political parties to select judges for appointment to the lower courts based upon political recommendations, and each party with a significant congressional presence would fight for its "quota" of appointments. The distribution of judiciary positions has been facilitated by the failure of the Judicial Council to institute the selection of judges on the basis of competitive exams as required by the Judicial Career Law of 1980, leaving the Council to appoint "temporary" judges — for whom no appointment criteria exist — or fill vacancies upon the non-public review of credentials of the candidates. The Judicial Council began

---

[88]Judicial appointments wére still governed by the Organic Law of the Judicial Power, adopted in 1956 under the dictatorship of General Marcos Pérez Jiménez. This Organic Law gave the Minister of Justice the right to appoint judges to the lower courts.

[89]Rogelio Pérez Perdomo, "Informe Sobre Venezuela" in Jorge Correa Sutil, ed., *Situación y Políticas Judiciales en América Latina* (Cuadernos de Análisis Jurídico, Escuela de Derecho Universidad Diego Portales, Santiago, Chile), at 567 [hereinafter Informe Sobre Venezuela]. Pérez Perdomo notes that the first president of the Judicial Council, a "prestigious independent jurist," resigned because he felt that his reputation was being used to legitimatize political agreements to divide up the judiciary among the parties. *Id.*

offering competitive exams in 1991, holding eighty competitions in 1991 and forty-four in 1992, but discontinued them again until 1995. As of 1991, approximately 52% of sitting "regular" judges had entered the judicial system without a competitive exam and a further 45% were "temporary" judges, many of whom had served in that status for more than ten years.[90]

The President. While Venezuela's Constitution nominally establishes independent executive, legislative and judicial branches, the executive in fact structurally dominates the judiciary. It does through its power to appoint the members of the Supreme Court (with confirmation by Congress) and one member of the Judicial Council, and its power over the budget — the Supreme Court, the Ministry of Justice, the Public Ministry and the Judicial Council must each negotiate an annual budget with the executive, who then presents these budget requests to the Congress. However, as one commentator has noted, the formal involvement of the executive and legislature in matters related to the judiciary does not suggest that the two branches serve as checks on each other's influence; the "independence" of each branch is "diluted by the fact that each is constituted by a majority of the same party and it is the party which ends up formulating the will of the state, submitting the judicial power to its private interests." [91]

Politics and the Supreme Court. The politicization of the Supreme Court has always been relatively open — the negotiations over appointments among the political parties were widely discussed in the press. The 1992 election of magistrates to the Supreme Court garnered intense publicity,

---

[90]Julio César Fernández Toro, *Estudio sobre el Nombramiento y Control de Magistrados, Jueces y Fiscales,* [mimeo] (1992), at 42 [hereinafter *El Nombramiento y Control de Magistrados*].

[91]*Id.,* at 41. This situation changed in the 1990s. Carlos Andrés Pérez faced considerable opposition from factions within his own party in the Congress. President Caldera was elected in December 1993 with only 30% of the vote. Congress was divided among several parties: AD won the most seats in the Senate (19) and the Chamber of Deputies (54); COPEI won 15 and 52, respectively; Convergencia picked up 5 and 24; Causa R, 9 and 40; and MAS, 5 Senators and 26 Deputies.

coming on the heels of a 1991 preliminary review by the Court of corruption charges brought against a former AD president, Jaimie Lusinchi (in office 1984-89).[92] The magistrate initially assigned the investigation of the charges, affiliated with the COPEI party, found sufficient evidence to proceed to trial. However, the majority of the court, affiliated with Lusinchi's AD party, rejected the opinion on an 8-7 party-line vote, and designated a new magistrate (with AD party affiliations) to review the evidence and prepare a new recommendation.[93] The closely-watched decision caused a political uproar, and led 29 distinguished academics and professionals, a group called *Los Notables* (the "Notable Ones"), to sign a letter in September 1991 requesting the resignation of the entire Supreme Court. The group argued the court had lost all legitimacy as a result of its politicization by the parties and called for revisions to the Constitution to strengthen the democratic institutions that no longer functioned as anticipated by the 1961 charter.

The unfolding of this drama was interrupted by a military coup attempt in February 1992. The overthrow attempt delayed the issuance of a new Lusinchi opinion until mid-1992 and dramatically altered the political climate — the corruption of the Venezuelan democracy by the political parties had been one of the justifications for the revolt. The new opinion found no evidence to support the corruption charges against Lusinchi. But the opinion was withdrawn only a few days after it was

---

[92]In Venezuela, charges brought against sitting or former presidents are filed with the Supreme Court. The Court first reviews the charges and evidence to determine whether a valid claim has been stated and sufficient evidence offered to warrant the charge. If the Court permits the case to go forward, the next step is a trial before the Court on the merits of the charge. The case against Lusinchi was at the preliminary stage, designated in Spanish as the *antejuicio de mérito*. If the Court found the charges to be grounded in evidence, the case would proceed to trial.

[93]It was rumored that ex-president Lusinchi had maneuvered the Court to give the investigation to a COPEI judge in order to turn the case into a clash between the two parties, which AD (and thus Lusinchi) was likely to win because of AD's majority on the Court.

issued by the magistrate who had written it, throwing the court into more confusion. Meanwhile, the terms of three magistrates were ending in 1992 and two more announced retirements. Given the crisis atmosphere and public clamor against corruption, the Congress broke with tradition and announced that the process for selecting the replacement justices would be public. The new openness quickly succumbed to the old maneuvering, however, as prestigious lawyers refused to serve, and the parties winced at loosing control of the highest court in the land. While the Congress ended up voting publicly for the new judges, AD and COPEI members (who, together, controlled majorities in each chamber) voted from a list agreed to beforehand by party leaders.

Conflict with Military Courts. A final source of conflict is the tendency of the military court system to ignore the jurisdiction and orders of civilian courts. This area is particularly troubling because of the long history of military dictatorship in Latin America (including Venezuela), whose effects still linger in the efforts of the high command of a number of states to insist on a special role for the armed forces in defending the constitution. Conflict between the military and civilian judiciaries erupted after the second coup attempt in November 1992, when a special *ad hoc* court martial was set up under the Code of Military Justice to try those accused of participating in the uprising. Civilians were subject to trial under its terms, even though the Constitution mandates that citizens are to be tried by their "natural" judges — in this case, civilian courts.[94] The Code dates from 1938, when Venezuela was governed by a military dictatorship, and a number of its provisions appear to be clearly unconstitutional and in violation of Venezuela's obligations under the International Covenant on Civil and Political Rights and the American

[94]Some 300 civilians were arrested in connection with the coup, held *incommunicado* and denied access to counsel for long periods. No formal charges were ever entered against them. A number of those arrested and later released without charges filed against them were prominent critics of the Pérez government.

Convention on Human Rights.[95] It provides for expedited trials, limiting the ability of the accused to gather evidence, and restricts access to counsel. The president has the authority to prohibit the trial of particular individuals and to order the suspension of a trial at any stage.

The *ad hoc* tribunals were declared unconstitutional by the Supreme Court in March 1993 on highly technical grounds. The court concluded that the emergency presidential decree establishing the tribunals did not suspend the right to be tried by one's natural judges (apparently interpreted to mean in this case the right to be tried in a court existing at the time of the alleged offense) and the right to an adequate defense. The cases were then remanded to the ordinary military courts for trial proceedings. Shortly thereafter, however, civilian judge Braulio Sánchez granted a writ of *habeas corpus* to a group of defendants who claimed they had been detained without formal charge for more than the prescribed eight days after their cases had been remanded to the ordinary military tribunals. The military court refused to comply with the order and announced that it would initiate judicial action against Judge Sánchez for "abuse of power" and "interfering with military justice." Sánchez' decision was upheld on appeal and the appellate judge, Luis Lecuna, ordered that a case be brought against the president of the military court for illegal deprivation of the liberty of the defendants. The growing crisis was defused in April when the Supreme Court agreed to decide the matter.[96]

---

[95]In 1994, the Inter-American Commission of Human Rights requested the government of Venezuela to derogate several sections of the Code. In an appearance before the Inter-American Court in February 1996, the government refused, asserting that the Code on its face did not violate any international norms.

[96]Over three years later, the Supreme Court has yet to issue an opinion in this case.

E. Corruption

Corruption is viewed as the most profound — and perhaps intractable — ill plaguing the courts. Every individual to whom we spoke and every article or study we reviewed identified corruption as either the most serious — or one of the most serious — issues in connection with legal reform. Newspaper stories document cases of alleged bribes and illicit influence on a regular basis.[97] A 1995 book, *¿Cuánto Vale un Juez?* ("How Much Does a Judge Cost?"), a compilation of old and more recent accusations of judicial corruption, created a stir and became a "best-seller" on the street.[98] A recent Minister of Justice, Ruben Creixems, has publicly quipped, in reference to the soaring crime rate in Caracas, that "[i]n Venezuela, it's important how much you rob, because you need to steal enough to pay bail and to corrupt the judge."[99]

Corruption takes many forms — daily "service fees" to obtain or process corporate or personal records; Christmas baskets of food and beverages given as gifts by lawyers and law firms to judges and administrative officials with whom they work; the use of the courts to intimidate political or business rivals; the request for bribes from judges and court personnel to assure a "balanced" (*i.e.*, not unduly influenced by the other party's payment) assessment of the facts of a case; the influence of political parties to decide outcomes for political or economic ends.

The Venezuelan example of corrupt clientelism *par excelence* is the judicial "tribe" — an informally organized network of judges, judicial

---

[97]In May 1995, for example, the press had a field day with the case of Mélida Aleksic Molina, a judge with thirty years of service on the bench. She had been removed from her tribunal after she was accused of extortion in a case before her court. When a police commissioner entered her apartment to arrest her, she tossed an estimated Bs 1,000,000 (US$6,000 at the then exchange rate) from her 10th floor balcony onto delighted pedestrians below.

[98]William Ojeda, *¿Cuánto Vale un Juez?* (Valencia, Venezuela: Editorial Vadell Hermanos, 1995). It also generated a number of defamation lawsuits.

[99]Jane Knight, "Frustrated With Crime, Vigilantes Roam Caracas," *Christian Science Monitor*, September 21, 1995, at 6.

personnel, private lawyers, elected and party officials dedicated to controlling a certain number of judges. The "tribe" guarantees the results of particular judicial proceedings in the hands of judges who are tribe members for an appropriate fee. The existence of these networks became fodder for the Venezuelan press during the crises of 1992; newspapers even presented organization charts of the most prominent tribes and their alleged members.

Corruption large and small is often facilitated by the structure of the courts. For example, in commercial and other civil law matters, fees are required for court services such as filing, copying or processing legal documents, and the speed and efficiency of the service often depend on the size of the "tip" added to the standard service charge. In the criminal area, on the other hand, a defendant under investigation in the initial phase of a penal matter may have no access to court files and the court proceedings are secret. The defendant may have no idea of the nature of the allegations or who has brought the charges (in Venezuela, individuals can request a court to open a criminal investigation). The secrecy and the fear of an arrest warrant and imprisonment in one of Venezuela's notorious prisons provide incentives for individuals to attempt to bribe judges through intermediaries.[100]

---

[100]Interview with attorneys, Caracas, May 1995. Venezuela's Code of Criminal Procedure *(Código de Enjuiciamiento Criminal)* divides a criminal case into two phases — the *sumario* (summary) and the *plenario* (plenary). The *sumario* is essentially a preliminary investigation conducted by the court to determine (i) if the charges levied against an individual state a violation of the criminal code, (ii) if the alleged events underlying the charges in fact occurred, and (iii) the identity of the person(s) responsible. This phase is conducted in secret and the defendant's only participatory right is to view the official court file (although file records cannot be copied for use in preparing a defense). If the court decides to prosecute, the trial shifts to the *plenario* stage, where proceedings are open and the defendant is entitled to all due process guarantees. The *sumario* procedure has been widely denounced as a violation of the right to a fair trial and due process. In June 1995, the Venezuelan House of Deputies unanimously agreed to eliminate the *sumario* in a bill revising the Code of Criminal Procedure. The new code is scheduled to be finalized and promulgated in 1996.

F. Institutional Neglect

Budget resources. The ability of the political parties to influence the judiciary is enhanced by the inadequate financial resources available to the Judicial Council. The original budget for the entire judiciary, Bs 8,379,000,000, absorbed only 0.7% of the national budget in 1994, as compared to three percent in 1958.[101] Additional credits throughout the year eventually raised this figure to Bs 13,379,000,000. The 1995 budget was projected at Bs 18,520,000,000; the executive initially cut the proposal by fifteen percent but restored the cuts and added credits to bring the sum to Bs 20,000,000,000.

The higher budget for 1995 did not reflect much of a real gain for the judiciary. The additional amount for 1995 barely kept pace with Venezuela's 65% inflation in 1994 (with an additional 60% in 1995) on top of a currency devaluation in 1994 of over 100% (and a further 70% decline in 1995). Thus, the judiciary gained enough funds to maintain its existing operations without adding any new tribunals or public defenders, real salary increases for judges or staff, or any expansion or improvement of administrative services.

The most serious casualty of these budgetary restrictions is the continuing need for large numbers of additional judges and the resulting increase in workloads and delays.

A second casualty is infrastructure. Courthouses generally are in poor physical condition, with judicial personnel crammed into small offices shared with the lawyers and their clients who have business before the court. Boxed files are ubiquitous, blocking hallways and filling storage rooms. Air conditioning, water, telephone and electrical systems often fail, when they are available at all. Supplies are very difficult to obtain. Modern office equipment is usually unavailable. Several judges told us they must buy supplies — pens, paper and erasers — and typewriters or

[101] *El Nombramiento y Control de Magistrados, supra* note 90, at 42. For comparative purposes, the Costa Rican Constitution stipulates that the judiciary must receive at least six percent of the national budget.

word processors with their own resources in order for the court to function.[102]

Judicial Salaries. Penurious judicial salaries constitute a widely-agreed upon source of both the low professional quality of many judges and a high incidence of corruption. A superior court judge with ten years of experience receives the equivalent of a US$600 monthly salary, out of which the judge must often purchase the supplies needed by the office. Real salaries in 1991 were 29% below the 1984 level; these already-low salaries were devastated by the 100% fall in the value of the Venezuelan currency in 1994, and continue to be battered by annual inflation in the range of 60 to 70%. Judicial salaries are based upon a civil service scale and are not determined through comparisons with the earnings of lawyers in private practice with similar experience.

The poor pay and working conditions takes its toll on judges interested in reform. One labor court judge resigned in May 1995, stating in his resignation letter that "the low pay received by judges and our staff does not allow us to meet our basic daily living requirements." He went on to note that "while low pay is not a valid excuse to justify corruption or irresponsibility in the exercise of the judicial function, it is indeed an obstacle to attracting and keeping the best lawyers for the administration of justice. . . ."[103]

Court Delays. The ability of the Judicial Council to oversee and administer the courts has been severely compromised over the last ten years. As the Bank analysis notes, "[t]he penal and civil courts are encountering serious case backlogs, procedural congestion, and judicial delays with the resulting effect of inefficient, costly and detrimental delivery of judicial services. These delays contribute to the appearance of

---

[102]Interviews with Judges, Caracas, May 1995. One judge suggested to us that he and his colleagues might have to ask corporations or foundations to donate equipment. To his credit, he quickly recognized the possible impropriety of his proposal.

[103]Interview with Luis Rafael Oquendo Rontondaro, Juez Cuarto de Primera Instancia del Trabajo, Caracas, May 1995.

impropriety and public perceptions that the courts are unresponsive, corrupt, and politically-influenced."[104]

The delays are extensive and affect the constitutional due process rights of those accused of crimes. The backlog at the trial court level increased fivefold between 1986-1991, resulting in an increase in the average processing time for criminal cases to 1,136 working days, 10.4 times the legal requirement set forth in the Code of Criminal Procedure.[105] Since bail is generally unavailable to the large number of poor defendants, persons accused of crimes usually wait in jail until guilt or innocence is determined. As of 1992, only an estimated 32% of the 30,000 people in prison had been actually sentenced, and, according to an estimate of the Attorney General's office, about thirteen percent of these prisoners would be found innocent.[106] Many of the accused spend more time in prison awaiting judicial processing of the case than that called for by the maximum penalty they could have received for the crime for which they are charged.

The delays affect all categories of cases before the courts, including those involving official corruption, constitutional matters and human rights. The list of well-known cases still pending includes the political corruption investigation of the bankruptcy of the Banco de Comercio (9.5 years); the massacre of fourteen fishermen by the army at El Amparo (7.5 years); the political and military abuses growing out of the suspension of guarantees in the wake of the February 1989 protests (7 years); the massacre of sixteen Yanomami Indians (2.5 years); the constitutional challenge to various provisions of the Code of Military Justice (2.5 years).

The record of the courts in matters implicating constitutionally-protected social, economic and cultural rights is no less troubling. In important cases affecting land and property rights, the Supreme Court has stalled. For example, a petition to declare

---

[104]World Bank, Venezuela Staff Appraisal Report, *supra* note 38, at 4.

[105]*Id.* Civil claims face similar delays — processing time averaged 783 working days, 4.4 times the legal requirement.

[106]*Id.*, at 8.

unconstitutional a municipal ordinance which declares extinct the indigenous community Kari'ña of Aguasaya and expropriates the community's lands had been pending before the Supreme Court since June 1989. The indigenous community has waited seven years for a response, during which time the cloud on the community's land titles has prevented it from obtaining loans and credits for farming. The members of the indigenous community have also been excluded from bilingual education programs.[107]

The failure of the courts to act expeditiously in land disputes between *campesinos* and large landholders has contributed to growing tensions in the countryside over the last several years, resulting in violent clashes which have left hundreds of *campesinos* injured and arrested, and several dead. When the courts have issued provisional orders in favor of the claims of the *campesinos,* the orders are ignored by the large landowners and peasants are ejected from parcels in dispute, at times with the assistance of the National Guard. The courts have never issued sanctions against those participating in the flagrant violation of judicial orders.[108]

Court Administration. The lack of proper court administration is reflected in archaic procedures, inadequate control mechanisms, duplication of effort, poor records management and weak administrative and logistical support to the judges. As a result, the Judicial Council's statistics fail to provide a complete picture of the problems and are of little use for improved court management and planning.[109] The Council's administrative capacity is greatly hindered by the lack of coordination in the Judicial Council itself — each magistrate is responsible for overseeing a particular management area, and each tends to guard that responsibility tightly. Continuity is a serious problem since all of the magistrates are

---

[107]Provea, *1990 Annual Report*, at 40; Provea, *1995 Annual Report*, at 87.

[108]Provea, *1993 Annual Report*, at 86.

[109]Venezuela Staff Appraisal Report, *supra* note 38, at 2-4.

usually replaced every five years.[110] And since the technical administrative staff of the Council is woefully lacking management skills,[111] institutional continuity is nonexistent.

More fundamentally, the judicial sector is administratively divided, its various components — the Supreme Court, the Public Ministry, the Judicial Council and the Justice Ministry — acting independently, each guarding its own prerogatives and rarely coordinating with the other judicial organs. The lack of cooperation derives from the politicization of the judicial sector, marked by the efforts of political and economic interests to gain control of each judicial organization. Thus, the judiciary as a whole remains impotent to counter the interventions of the executive and legislative branches, which render its autonomy and independence precarious.

G. Outdated Legal Codes

Legislative reform of the laws governing the several sectors of the judiciary is long overdue — the Congress has passed new judiciary laws which conflict with or derogate sections of already existing laws without making the statutes consistent. For example, the 1980 Judicial Career Law partially derogated the 1956 Organic Law of the Judicial Power and the 1969 Partial Reform of the Organic Law of the Judicial Power. Then in 1987 the entire (1956) Organic Law of the Judicial Power was replaced by a new code of the same name. In 1988, Congress adopted the Organic Law of the Judicial Council which, in turn, revoked sections of the 1987 Organic Law of the Judicial Power and the 1988 Judicial Career Law. The

---

[110]The consequences of which were felt by the World Bank when the entire Judicial Council was replaced between the time the project was approved by the Bank's Board and the time the project was administratively ready to go forward. *See* below at 85-86.

[111]One of the unpleasant surprises encountered by the Bank as it was beginning the implementation stage of the Project was the inability of the Council staff to handle the most elementary managerial tasks, such as establishing and managing dedicated bank accounts or hiring outside consultants.

Commercial Code, the Civil Code, the Code of Civil Procedure and the Code of Criminal Procedure date from early this century.[112]

H. Access to Justice for the Poor

Access to the formal mechanisms of justice in Venezuela is highly restricted, particularly for those with few economic resources. Few alternative forums — which may be preferable because they cost less and are faster — exist.[113] A promising new forum for the poor is the justice of the peace, inaugurated in 1994. Rogelio Pérez Perdomo, an academic who studies judicial systems, cautions, however, that these mechanisms are not useful for ensuring that the state complies with human rights norms.[114]

The formal, written nature of Venezuela's civil law system — the requirements for following proper procedures and filing properly drafted documents — combined with administrative chaos means that any significant legal matter requires the assistance of an attorney. Most of Venezuela's vast poor population cannot afford to hire legal counsel and therefore access to the legal system is effectively closed.

Public Defenders. Venezuelan law provides for public defenders in criminal matters for those unable to afford an attorney. The public defender system, however, is hampered by several problems. First, there are not enough public defenders to handle the caseload.[115] In 1993, for

[112]Problems with the 1938 Code of Military Justice are discussed above at 54-55.

[113]Traditional alternative dispute resolution mechanisms include arbitration, conciliation and informal local courts.

[114]Informe Sobre Venezuela, *supra* note 89, at 583.

[115]Venezuelan jurisprudence divides the government-provided lawyers into three general classes: those who provide counsel in criminal matters are called "public defenders" (*defensores públicos*); those relating to labor and minors are called "labor and juvenile prosecutors" (*procuradores de trabajadores y menores*), and those working for rural and indigenous populations, "agrarian prosecutors"

example, 157 public defenders shared a total of 45,702 cases, an average of 291 cases per lawyer.[116] The Judicial Council estimated that it needed a minimum of 84 additional public defenders for 1994 to meet national needs, but only two lawyers were hired.[117] The ratio of cases per lawyer subsequently increased to 348 in 1995. In several states, the 1995 average was 450 cases per lawyer; in the state of Sucre, that number jumped to 625.[118]

Second, the 1980 Judicial Career Law contemplated the promulgation of a separate code creating and governing a Public Defender Institution.[119] That code has yet to be drafted, though, leaving the public defender without a set of norms establishing the office's institutional role in relation to judges and other court officials. Partially as result of this institutional limbo, the organizational culture of the public defender system generates strong biases against the interests of the system's clients. Public defenders are technically employees of the Ministry of Justice.[120] Organizationally, however, they function as an arm of the Judicial Council, often sharing offices with judges and court personnel.

Provea was involved in a case in the state of Delta Amaruco in 1995 in which an indigenous woman was found guilty in a criminal matter and sentenced to six months in prison (after having spent three years in prison awaiting trial). Provea asked the public defender in the case to file an

---

(*procuradores agrarios*). Unless otherwise noted, all will be included under the term "public defender."

[116]Provea, *1994 Annual Report*, at 80.

[117]Judicial Council, *Memoria y Cuenta 1993*, at 6.

[118]Provea, *1995 Annual Report*, at 88.

[119]*See* Judicial Career Law, Article 73.

[120]The *procuradores de trabajadores* are named by the Labor Minister and are employees of the Ministry of Labor; the *procuradores de menores* are appointed by the Public Prosecutor and work for the Public Ministry. Finally, the *procuradores agrarios* are selected by the President and work for the Ministry of Agriculture.

appeal. This appeal greatly irritated the criminal court judge, who interpreted the action as disloyalty to the court group on the part of the public defender. The judge viewed the action as a possible black mark on her judicial career, since appeals by public defenders are so rare.

Third, Pérez Perdomo reports that public defenders generally "sense a great social distance between themselves and their clients, view them as guilty and clearly are not disposed to make any effort to defend them."[121] Much of this situation seems to derive from the social status of the public defender, whose position "is not accepted as a desirable job, except for the little effort that it is assumed to require."[122] Pérez Perdomo relates an interview with a president of the Judicial Council who said he had recommended the job of public defender to a young attorney who had recently given birth to a child because the position's light workload would not interfere with family obligations. Another public defender was a former judge who had suffered a heart attack and gave up the judicial post under medical advice for "less stressful" work.[123] The resulting quality of defense is predictable:

> Contact between defendants and public defenders is so superficial that many interviewed prisoners ignore the fact that they have public counsel and when asked about the role of the public defender at court hearings where the presence of counsel is required, the prisoners make no distinctions among the roles [of the judge and public defender]; rather, all of the judicial functionaries are viewed together as "those who want to screw [the prisoners]."[124]

---

[121]Informe Sobre Venezuela, *supra* note 89, at 588.

[122]*Id.*

[123]*Id.*

[124]*Id.*

Access to justice is particularly critical in a judicial system where the administrative capacity to manage prisoners has collapsed and bail as such is not available to those accused of lesser crimes. Inmates without financial resources can easily become "forgotten prisoners" if they do not have an attorney continuously monitoring the court's actions. The stories of prisoners lost within the justice system are often astounding: an investigation by the Andean Commission of Jurists in 1992 turned up, among the most egregious examples, a person detained for fourteen months before the police even notified the court of the arrest; two individuals sentenced to three years in prison who actually served over ten years; a prisoner who spent seventeen years in the penitentiary never having been convicted or sentenced by a court; and an individual sentenced to fourteen months who ended up detained for over nine years.[125]

Court Fees. The cost of litigation is the major barrier for the poor. While district and municipal courts are competent to hear claims in disputes involving relatively small amounts of money, the poor tend not to use the courts for financial disputes. This is particularly true in states like Venezuela, where 73% of the population live below the official poverty line (and 43% in critical poverty, unable to earn enough to feed a family). The disputes which lead low-income persons to court involve family, labor and land, all matters under the jurisdiction of the civil courts of first instance. These courts have set fees for all judicial services which are presently beyond the means of the great majority of the population.

According to research carried out by the Federal District (Caracas) Bar Association (*Colegio de Abogados del Distrito Federal*) prior to the implementation of fee increases in 1994, only fourteen percent of the population could afford to use the courts.[126] In May 1996, the minimum monthly wage in the private sector stood at Bs 45,000 (US$90). Yet the court fee to file a criminal complaint (in a case where the accuser is not

---

[125]Andean Commission of Jurists, *Venezuela: Administración de Justicia y Crisis Institucional Venezuela* (Lima, Peru: 1992), at 86-87.

[126]Provea, *1994 Annual Report*, at 84.

physically hurt) is Bs 10,000 (US$20); to file a witness affidavit, Bs 1,000 (US$2); for the issuance of an interlocutory decree, Bs 2,500 (US$5); for the issuance of a final judgment, Bs 3,500 (US$7); for the performance of an autopsy, between Bs 5,000 and 10,000 (US$5-10). In the civil and commercial courts, fees are similarly high: the filing fee for a divorce is Bs 1,500 (US$3); for the reading of a will, Bs 6,000 (US$12); to incorporate a company, Bs 5,000 (US$5); to grant a power of attorney, between Bs 500 and 1,000 (US$1-2).

These statutory fees are augmented by the extralegal "fees" requested by court administrative personnel for most basic services. In addition, the courts of first instance are concentrated in Caracas and the regional capitals, forcing the population living outside urban centers to absorb the cost of travel as well. Pérez Perdomo notes this restrictive policy "is not explicit [or formal] but is coherent with other actions and regulations which permit one to call this result a true policy and not an undesired circumstance or the perverse effect of other measures."[127]

Alternative Dispute Resolution: The Justice of the Peace. In December 1994 the Venezuelan Congress partially offset the new fee burdens by creating a new alternative dispute resolution route for the poor, the Justice of the Peace (*Juez de Paz*).[128] The new community-based courts of equity will provide informal means for resolving local conflicts, principally through mediation. Difficulties are anticipated, however, over subject matter jurisdiction and the capacity of the new judges to carry out the informal dispute resolution objective of the court in a fair manner — judges (who do not have to be lawyers) are to receive only sixty hours of basic training. Other possible sources for mediation include the Legal Aid Section of the Municipality of Caracas (for neighborhood housing

---

[127]Informe Sobre Venezuela, *supra* note 89, at 585.

[128]Justice of the peace legislation was actually first adopted in 1993 (*Ley Orgánica de Tribunales y Procedimientos de Paz*), but serious problems led to the 1994 redrafting of the bill (now known as the *Ley Orgánica de Justicia de Paz*).

disputes), labor boards and offices at municipal and regional levels of government.[129]

I. Conclusion

This chapter has attempted to provide an overview of the range of interrelated problems characterizing Venezuela's judicial sector. While noting the seriousness of the administrative and management problems resulting from years of institutional neglect and the lack of judicial training — areas the Project specifically targets — it emphasized the extraordinary corrosion of the judicial function brought about by extensive political interference and corruption — areas neither the Bank, the Judicial Council, the Congress or the President have yet to credibly address. The most egregious manifestation of the collapse of the judicial sector, beyond the disdain for the courts reflected in the citizenry, has been the wholesale eclipse of the fundamental role of judges in the protection of the human rights of Venezuelan citizens. And while the institutional state of the judiciary has contributed to that failure, the larger problem lies with judges whose meager qualifications or political commitments hinder the ability of citizens to hold the government accountable and the inability of the Public Ministry and the Ministry of Justice to fulfill their duties to bring those responsible to the courts for trial.

---

[129]*See* Rogelio Pérez Perdomo, "Asistencia jurídica y acceso a la justicia en Venezuela" in Pérez Perdomo, ed., *Justicia y pobreza en Venezuela* (Caracas, Venezuela: Monte Avila, 1987).

III. Human Rights In Venezuela

President Carlos Andrés Pérez launched his dramatic change in Venezuelan economic policy in late 1989 by reducing government subsidies for public services, removing tariffs on imports and opening the formerly state-directed economy to international trade. The resulting increases in prices and reduction of social spending set off public protests and riots which were violently repressed by the military, leaving hundreds dead.

The killings focused the world's attention on the increasingly perilous human rights situation in Venezuela. By 1992, the list of problems had become lengthy. The United States Department of State noted the persistent "arbitrary and excessively lengthy detentions, abuse of detainees, extrajudicial killings by the police and military, the failure to punish police and security officers accused of abuses, corruption and gross inefficiency in the judicial and law enforcement systems, deplorable prison conditions, a lack of respect for the rights of indigenous people, and violence and discrimination against women."[130] The Venezuelan constitutional mechanisms designed to protect human rights — the courts and the Public Prosecutor — failed to take appropriate steps to hold government agents and agencies accountable and the resulting impunity only fueled the ongoing abuses.

A. The Explosion of Human Rights Violations

In recent years, the Venezuelan security forces have been accused of serious human rights violations.[131] Provea documented 80 extrajudicial

---

[130]United States Department of State, *Country Reports on Human Rights Practices for 1994*, at 520.

[131]Venezuela's Constitution protects a comprehensive list of civil, political, social and economic rights. Guarantees include, among others, the right to life (Article 58); protection against warrantless searches and detentions (Articles 60.1 and 62), torture or other physical or mental abuse (Article 60.3); the right to peaceful protest (Article 115) and free expression (Article 66); prohibition of discrimination (Article 61); the right to petition the government and receive a reply (Article 67); the right of access to justice and the right to an

killings by security forces in 1991, 143 in 1992, 187 in 1993, 148 in 1994 and 126 in 1995. There were 13,941 arbitrary detentions between October 1994 and September 1995. The use of torture as a normal investigation technique is widespread, as noted by the 99 cases reported last year, a number above the 1991-95 annual average of 67.[132] Repression of non-violent protests by the security forces is now routine. Horrible prison conditions abetted by poorly trained prison guards combined to produce massacres of 34 and 100 inmates in separate incidents in 1993 and 1994. Approximately 274 individuals were killed in prison violence in 1995, 498 died in 1994, 195 in 1993, 220 in 1992 and 124 in 1991.[133]

Recent Venezuelan presidents returned to a tradition of suspending constitutional guarantees whenever an economic or political crisis appears. President Carlos Andrés Pérez suspended guarantees after each of the 1992 coup attempts.[134] Just as troubling was President Caldera's June 27, 1994 suspension of several constitutional guarantees — the protections against warrantless searches and arrest; the expropriation of property without compensation and the rights to freedom of movement, own private property and freely engage in any economic activity — allegedly to address the *economic* crisis triggered by the collapse of the banking sector. The Congress, pursuant to its constitutional prerogative, almost immediately revoked the President's emergency decree. In a test

---

adequate defense (Article 68); the right to be tried by one's "natural" judges (Article 69); and the right to challenge the constitutionality of a court's actions (*amparo*) (Article 49). In addition, Venezuela is a signatory to and has incorporated into its domestic law the norms contained in the International Covenant on Civil and Political Rights and the American Convention on Human Rights.

[132]*See* Provea, *1995 Annual Report*, at 24.

[133]*Id*; Provea, *1994 Annual Report*, at 247; *1993 Annual Report*, at 87; *1992 Annual Report*, at 63; *1991 Annual Report*, at 57.

[134]*See* the discussion of the aftermath of the second coup attempt below at 76.

of political wills, Caldera then re-issued the decree the next day and threatened to seek a referendum on the issue if the Congress moved to revoke his powers again. The Congress backed down and the suspensions endured until July 1995.

Although the suspension of guarantees was based on an alleged need to investigate and arrest the bankers accused of fraud in the collapse of the banking sector in February 1994,[135] the government

> profited from the suspension to take aggressive actions far removed from the economic sphere. After the suspension, the police conducted numerous raids in poor urban areas of Caracas. Along with poor youths — a common target of these raids — social activists, popular leaders, and members of leftist parties were searched and detained arbitrarily, and often held incommunicado. During the month of July, for example, Provea reported that 1,995 persons had been detained in police raids, of which only 42 had been sought for the commission of crimes. In September, according to Inter Press Service, 1,600 police and military officers carried out an enormous raid of housing projects in a poor urban area west of Caracas, affecting some 10,000 families. Indeed, rather than a focused effort to resolve the economic crisis, it appeared that the suspension of guarantees facilitated an unrestricted fight against crime, urban violence and social unrest.[136]

---

[135]Most of Venezuela's private banks collapsed in 1994, leading the government to inject approximately $6 billion (16% of GNP) in an effort to stem the insolvency crisis. The collapse was triggered by the surprise closing of Banco Latino, the country's largest bank, and the subsequent flight of many of the bank's directors and principal managers from Venezuela as charges of massive fraud surfaced. This scenario repeated itself with the succeeding failure of up to 80% of the private banking sector. Caldera ostensibly sought emergency powers to prevent the flight of bank owners and officers and the transfer out of the country of bank and personal assets they controlled.

[136]Human Rights Watch, *World Report 1994* (1995), at 721-722.

The police assault on poor neighborhoods in Caracas has continued for several years, justified in part by a "loitering" statute, the Law on Vagrants and Delinquents, which gives the security forces the right to arrest and imprison for up to five years individuals on the street suspected of being "vagrants" or "delinquents." The law has been widely criticized by domestic and international human rights organizations as unconstitutionally vague and a violation of due process rights.

The economic and social rights of Venezuelans have also deteriorated significantly during this period, particularly following the launch in 1989 of the World Bank/IMF-assisted structural adjustment program.[137] Several years of high inflation, currency devaluation and diminishing government social spending have contributed to a dramatic rise in poverty and its attendant social and health ills. The value of the average Venezuelan salary fell 53% in real terms from December 1993 to July 1995. At the same time, the poverty level has risen to include 73% of the population. More critically, 43% of the population does not earn enough money to cover the minimum monthly costs for food and housing for a family of six. In 1995, the official unemployment rate was 11.5%, a number which did not include the 45% of the working population active in the informal economy. A housing shortage has reached one million units, suggesting that more than six million people (assuming an average family size of six members) have no home or live in unsanitary conditions.

While the percentage of the national budget dedicated to debt repayment jumped from 20% in 1989 to over 40% in 1995, the percentage dedicated to social programs has fallen to 1%. Budget reductions have also affected the nation's health. With 71% of national

---

[137]*See generally* Provea, *1995 Annual Report,* at 111-198. The government's commitment to protect the social and economic rights is guaranteed by Venezuela's Constitution and the International Covenant on Economic, Social and Cultural Rights, to which Venezuela is a signatory. Guarantees under the Venezuelan Constitution include health protection and maintenance (Article 76), protection of indigenous populations (Article 77), the right to education (Article 78), guarantees related to employment and working conditions (Articles 84-92), social security (Article 94), the right to own private property (Article 99) and the protection of the state's natural resources (Article 106).

health expenditures aimed at hospitals and only 13% at primary and preventative care, illnesses once thought eradicated are reappearing, and a drop in vaccination programs has led to an increase in infant mortality. Public hospitals and clinics do not have the resources to serve the poor — the facilities themselves are in poor physical condition, there is a shortage of supplies and funds to pay medical salaries are scarce. Finally, of the nine principal nutrition indicators analyzed by the National Institute of Nutrition, only two meet minimum acceptable standards.

The failure to protect land rights has generated social conflicts in the countryside, particularly between indigenous citizens and ranchers. No reliable registers of land titles exist for parcels included in agrarian land reform programs; almost 73% of indigenous landholders do not possess any official title.

In addition, environmental policies are driven by the economic goal to generate mineral and timber wealth, and the effects of efforts to develop these natural resources on the environment have not been adequately assessed, even though impact studies are required by Venezuelan law. For example, although more than 80% of Venezuela's uncontaminated rivers and 74% of its forests are in the states of Bolívar and Amazonas, some 40 foreign companies have been authorized by the government to develop large-scale extractive mining operations, principally for gold and diamonds. It has been estimated that mining operations now underway in Bolivar State release some 1,250 kilograms of mercury annually into the watershed for the Caroní River, one of the country's largest sources of fresh water.

All of these conditions serve to increase social unrest, as well as the possibility of inappropriate or excessive reaction by governmental authorities. An accessible and fair judicial system in which legal disputes on social and economic rights issues can be resolved would undoubtedly reduce tensions that lead to other rights violations.

B. Impunity and the Judicial Sector

These violations of the human rights of Venezuelan citizens have continued unabated in recent years in large part because those officials responsible have acted with *de facto* impunity. For example, no one has been held responsible for the hundreds of civilians killed during the civil disturbances of 1989 or the deaths of over a thousand prisoners since 1990. Only a handful of low-ranking officers have been held responsible for 684 extrajudicial killings by the security forces over the past five years. Nor has Venezuela complied with the order of the Inter-American Commission on Human Rights to investigate and punish the members of the military responsible for, and compensate the families of the victims of an army massacre of fourteen fishermen in the village of El Amparo in 1988.[138]

The problems giving rise to the ability of members of the police and military to act outside legal norms without fear of punishment range across the judicial sector.

> The police often fail to investigate crimes that they or their law enforcement colleagues allegedly committed, and the judicial system remains highly inefficient and sometimes corrupt. A special pretrial summary phase called the "nudo hecho," used in cases involving public officials, often shields members of the

---

[138]The tortured legal history of the effort to determine responsibility for the 1988 massacre is reviewed in Provea's *Annual Reports* from 1989 to 1995 and Human Rights Watch/Americas, *Human Rights in Venezuela* (October 1993) at 20-30. The army claimed that the fishermen were armed guerrillas, but the evidence indicated otherwise. The army sought to cover up the killings despite the efforts of the families of the victims and human rights groups to bring the truth to light. After several years of controversial military and civilian court proceedings, the case was taken to the Inter-American Court of Human Rights. That court initiated formal proceedings against Venezuela in January 1994. In March, the Venezuelan Foreign Minister acknowledged official responsibility for the massacre and committed the government to pay damages. However, to date, no settlement has been reached. Human Rights Watch concluded that "[m]uch of the responsibility for this state of affairs lay with the [Venezuelan] judicial system. Civilian courts were plagued by politicization, corruption, inefficiency, and lack of resources; military courts were not impartial and were subject to a high degree of executive control." Human Rights Watch, *World Report 1995*, at 120.

security forces from prosecution, as a case can languish in that phase for several years. In addition, military courts are often strongly biased in favor of members of the armed forces accused of abuse. In the small number of prosecutions in which the military courts convict perpetrators of extrajudicial killings and other abuses, the sentences issued are frequently light, or, more commonly, the convictions are overturned on appeal. Unlike common prisoners, members of the security forces charged with crimes rarely spend time in prison.[139]

1. Role of The Public Ministry

The Public Ministry has a broad constitutional mandate to protect human rights in Venezuela, but much of the Ministry's actual work has consisted of denunciations of alleged human rights violations without initiating follow-up investigations or legal actions. The Public Ministry is principally responsible for requesting a court to investigate public officials (including the police) charged with abuse. The Public Prosecutor requests a court to open an *averiguación de nudo hecho*, an expedited procedure aimed at protecting officials from baseless accusations. In practice, however, the procedure promotes impunity. The objective of this preliminary investigation is simply to determine if the accused public official was a state agent on active duty when the alleged illegal act occurred and whether the act as alleged would constitute a crime.[140] If the Public Prosecutor does decide to file charges at the completion of this preliminary investigation, the agent must be removed from duty and turned over to the jurisdiction of the courts. The public official is entitled to remain free and to continue working until the procedure terminates.

---

[139]United States Department of State, *Country Reports on Human Rights Practices for 1994*, at 520. *See also* Human Rights Watch, *World Report 1995*, at 120.

[140]Circular of the Public Ministry (DH-1-CIRCULAR-8-76), December 8, 1976.

The Public Prosecutor has broad discretion not to file charges if it believes the complaint does not state a claim or if the evidence is clearly insufficient.

Although they should take no more than a few weeks "*nudo hecho* investigations can languish for years. The investigation, which is conducted in secret, can be delayed by uncooperative police [or] indifferent or recalcitrant judges . . . and neither the State Prosecutor nor the victim has legal means to force them to act." Since the investigation can be prolonged in this manner, the temporary immunity which the official enjoys during the *nudo hecho* process "can become permanent in those not infrequent cases in which the statute of limitations runs out before the *nudo hecho* investigation concludes and criminal charges can be brought."[141]

In at least eleven cases of torture and extrajudicial killings denounced by the Network of Support for Justice and Peace (*Red de Apoyo por la Justicia y la Paz*), a human rights NGO, Ministry lawyers decided not to initiate an *averiguación de nudo hecho,* in spite of the clear obligation of the Ministry to do so.[142] In the aftermath of the November 1992 coup attempt (which allegedly involved civilians), Ministry lawyers failed to investigate the detentions of those accused of participating in the uprising for twelve days after the event, again in spite of the Ministry's clear legal duty to do so in the face of widespread reports that those arrested were held (unconstitutionally) incommunicado and subjected to abuse and torture.

The situation had become so problematic that in 1995 the Public Prosecutor finally circulated a memorandum to the prosecutors and public defenders of the Public Ministry emphasizing the need for compliance

---

[141]Human Rights Watch/Americas, *Human Rights in Venezuela* (1993), at 16.

[142]*See* Red de Apoyo por la Justicia y la Paz, *Venezuela: Horror e Impunidad, Inventario No. 1* (Caracas, 1994) [hereinafter *Horror e Impunidad*]. The Public Ministry has an office dedicated to this responsibility and includes in its annual report a summation of the status of *averiguaciones de nudo hecho* actions filed by the Ministry.

with the ten-day limitation for completing the *nudo hecho* proceeding.[143] The contrast with the actual time periods required to complete the process as revealed by a report on the *nudo hecho* cases initiated by the *Red de Apoyo* is stark — a minimum of seven weeks (five times the legal limit) and a maximum of three years.[144]

At times when the Public Prosecutor has initiated prison inspections, lack of follow-up has been commonplace. In one particularly egregious example, the Public Prosecutor sent 78 memoranda to the Director of Prisons in the Ministry of Justice in a three-month period, denouncing the horrid conditions of the penitentiaries. In spite of the fact that not one of these missives was answered, the Public Prosecutor took no judicial action to force the Ministry to comply with its constitutional duty.

The Public Prosecutor has received commendations for the celebrated investigation of the charges of corruption brought against former President Carlos Andrés Pérez. But, as a magistrate of the Supreme Court of Spain noted after a visit with Amnesty International in 1993, the Fiscalía's actions against a sitting president only served to "call attention to the fact that the Public Ministry does not have the same ability to bring a case against a policeman on the beat."[145]

2. *The Role of the Ministry of Justice*

The Ministry of Justice administers the nation's prison system, which has been described as one of the worst in Latin America. In spite of Ministry efforts, the proportion of prisoners awaiting trial and those already convicted and serving a sentence has not changed — of 24,995 inmates as of November 1, 1995, only 7,450 (30%) had been convicted

---

[143]Fiscalía General de la República, *Informe del Fiscal General de la República 1994*, at 24.

[144]*Horror e Impunidad, supra* note 142, at 120.

[145]José Antonio Martin Pallin, Remarks at a Press Conference at the Completion of Amnesty International's Mission to Venezuela, May 1993.

of a crime.[146] Corruption affects the ability of prisoners to get to court. In February 1995, the Catia prison (approximately 1,000 inmates) had only one bus to transport prisoners to courts in the Caracas metropolitan area. Allegedly, the price of a seat on the bus for the trip to court was Bs 10,000.[147] Prisons remain plagued by violence, corruption and a serious lack of health and social services.[148]

The Ministry also directs the Judicial Technical Police (*Policía Técnica Judicial*), a national police force responsible for investigating crimes and collecting evidence to be used in criminal proceedings. The PTJ, as it is commonly called, has been widely criticized for delays in collecting and submitting evidence to the courts and for manipulating evidence in cases brought against members of the security forces. The most notorious example of manipulation of evidence was revealed with the opening of the court files in the five-year struggle to hold accountable the members of the security forces involved in the massacre of fourteen fishermen at El Amparo. After reviewing the file, Provea concluded that "most of the [length and outcome] of the process culminating in the Court Martial's absurd decision [exonerating all members of the security forces of any culpability] is due to the systematic effort of the PTJ to distort, forge and hide evidence in order to protect members of the PTJ who participated in the massacre."[149] The PTJ's forensic pathologists have been accused of

---

[146]Information provided to Provea by the *Dirección General Sectorial de Defensa y Protección Social del Ministerio de Justicia*, in a communication dated November 9, 1995.

[147]Provea, *1995 Annual Report*, at 101.

[148]*See generally* Provea, *1995 Annual Report*, at 97-110.

[149]Provea, *1993 Annual Report*, at 82. Other examples abound. Although Thais Roldan was killed by the National Guard in November 1993, the prosecutor in the case has yet to formally indict the security agents involved since she had not received the results of ballistics tests carried out by the PTJ. A similar situation prevails in a case involving a student who was almost killed when the (Caracas) Metropolitan Police attempted to suppress a peaceful protest in May 1994 — no prosecution has been initiated because the Commander of the Metropolitan Police has not provided a list of the names of the police who

acting negligently in the performance of autopsies and delaying the collection of evidence in cases involving public officials and members of the security forces.[150] The manipulation of evidence and mishandling of autopsies in cases against members of the security forces continues the atmosphere of impunity that permits police agents to act without consideration for the human rights of Venezuelan citizens.

The failure of the PTJ to act also affects the ability of the courts to move forward in cases involving social rights. In mid-1994, for example, an explosion at the state-owned petrochemical plant, Complejo Petroquímica at El Tablazo, caused extensive harm to the semi-rural community of El Hornito. The case could lead to penal sanctions against the responsible party. Nevertheless, the PTJ has yet to conclude the technical reports necessary for the initiation of a judicial investigation.

---

participated in the attack on the students. Provea, *1995 Annual Report*, at 94. In a third example, family members of a Carabobo State Police officer who had been shot by PTJ agents were detained and threatened by the PTJ investigators on the case as they tried to take the dying policeman to the hospital. The PTJ agents tried to change the policeman's pistol and place drugs on his body after it arrived at the hospital, apparently to justify what might have been a murder to prevent testimony against a PTJ agent involved in the drug trade. Provea, *1994 Annual Report*, at 87.

[150]Red de Apoyo por la Justicia y Paz, *Venezuela: Horror e Impunidad, Inventario No. 2* (Caracas, 1994), at 100.

IV. The Struggle For Reform

A. Venezuelan Reform Initiatives Prior to the Project

Judicial reform had been nominally on the Venezuelan political agenda for a number of years prior to the development of the World Bank Project. In 1984, then-President Lusinchi created an independent research institute to develop proposals for the modernization of the Venezuelan state and to draft the legislation and constitutional changes necessary to permit the implementation of the recommendations. The resulting Presidential Commission for the Reform of the State (*Comisión Presidencial para la Reforma del Estado*: COPRE) gave high priority to the judicial sector, noting at the outset of its work that "the most important step to strengthen the rule of law is the revitalization of the Judicial Power as the arbitrator and regulator consecrated in the structure of the democratic system."[151] In 1989, the Congress revived a long-dormant Special Bicameral Commission for the Revision of the Constitution in order to produce proposals for a broad overhaul of the charter.

In 1990, COPRE published a report, *Strengthening the Rule of Law,* which set forth detailed recommendations for judicial administrative and code reform.[152] The institute then created a judicial reform committee, comprised of representatives of the judiciary institutions (the Supreme Court, the Judicial Council, the Fiscalía General and the Ministry of Justice), bar associations and COPRE, which met every fifteen days during 1990 to draft legislation to implement the report's principal recommendations. The committee's main product was legislation that sought to rationalize the various codes governing the functioning of the judicial system — codes establishing the functional norms of the Judiciary

---

[151]Comisión Presidencial para la Reforma del Estado, *La Reforma del Estado, Proyecto de Reforma Integral del Estado*, vol. 1 (Caracas, Venezuela: Editorial Arte, 1988), at 55.

[152]Comisión Presidencial para la Reforma del Estado, *La Reforma del Estado, Fortalecimiento del Estado de Derecho*, vol. 5 (Caracas, Venezuela: Editorial Arte, 1990).

Council, the regulations for a legal career, the establishment of a justice of the peace, and the rules for the Supreme Court. Bills were introduced into the Congress in 1990 but were immediately tabled by opposition to judicial reform and the political crisis triggered by President Carlos Andrés Pérez' economic reforms.

Frustrated by the lack of congressional support, the COPRE committee decided to pursue administrative reforms through the Judicial Council, which would not require legislative approval. The Council began requiring the selection of new judges by open competition in 1991 in an effort to reduce political influence and increase the quality of new appointees. The Council also moved to decentralize its operations, creating regional judicial councils throughout the country. The reform committee also considered seeking grants for reform initiatives from European foundations. Then discussions with the Bank began.

B. The Bank and Venezuelan Reform

1. The Scope of Reform

The Venezuela Judicial Reform Project grew out of the Bank's involvement in the macroeconomic restructuring program initiated by Carlos Andrés Pérez at the outset of his Presidency in 1989. At the request of the Pérez government, the Bank negotiated structural adjustment and trade policy loans with Venezuela in 1989, followed by three additional loans in 1990 aimed at sectoral and institutional changes necessary to support private sector development. Aware that the Bank had supported reform of legislative procedures in Chile, Moises Naím, Venezuela's World Bank representative at the time, suggested to CORDIPLAN, the government's planning agency, the possibility of approaching the Bank for support for reform of the judiciary.

CORDIPLAN discussed the idea with the Judicial Council and COPRE and the parties agreed to seek Bank funding.[153]

The Bank was initially hesitant, for reasons discussed earlier — judicial reform was an area in which it had little institutional experience, having modestly funded technical support in training, the purchase of word processing equipment, the strengthening of legal information systems and the establishment of specialized commercial courts. In addition, the Bank was concerned that certain components of legal reform — judicial selection and training, the constitutional structure of the judicial power, the content of legal codes and the enforcement of legal norms (commercial or political) — would involve the Bank in issues of particular sensitivity to state sovereignty.[154] Finally, both the Bank and CORDIPLAN had doubts about the ability of the Judicial Council — or any other judicial sector entity — to manage a large project.

Thus, the scope of the project became the critical issue in the discussions. COPRE and a number of Pérez' ministers wanted a Bank-supported project to include legislative reform of legal codes and the organizational statutes of the judicial sector entities and to involve the Supreme Court, the Ministry of Justice and the Fiscalía.[155] Given its own institutional worries and the administrative limitations of the Venezuelan government, the Bank insisted on a project of limited scope aimed at improving the management and operation of the judicial system and the training of judges. Reform, therefore, shifted to matters of administration and training. A revitalized judiciary would have to be built from the ground up, "accelerat[ing] modernization without waiting for new laws, which can be prepared in parallel; accomplishing reforms with existing

---

[153]Interview with Pedro Miguel Reyes, President of the Judicial Council from 1989-1994, Caracas, May 1995; Interview with a staff member of CORDIPLAN during the Pérez' administration, Caracas, May 1995.

[154]*See* discussion above at 26-27.

[155]Pedro Miguel Reyes, *Venezuela y su experiencia en los programas de reforma judicial* (Paper delivered at the World Bank Conference on Judicial Reform in Latin America and the Caribbean, Washington, D. C., June 13-14, 1994), at 7-8.

legislation; and making tribunals more flexible. . . . Reforming the tribunal should then generate the conditions for legislative change."[156] The reform project became a gamble that changes in court and case management, if successful, would serve to stimulate broader reforms later.

Although limited in scope, the project attracted opposition. A number of political leaders argued that Bank involvement would violate Venezuelan judicial autonomy and compromise national sovereignty. The judiciary itself was divided — many judges preferred that any Bank loan agreement be directed at addressing current operating needs (salaries, equipment, courthouse improvements) while others rejected structural changes and argued for an expansion of the number of courts and judges as the way to overcome judicial deficiencies. More problematic was the opposition generated by the political parties with vested interests in control of the courts and institutional jealousy among the several arms of the judicial system over access to and management of the loan resources.[157]

Regardless of concerns over possible opposition, the Bank and the Judicial Council came to terms on the structure of the project in late 1991. The Bank conducted a preparation mission in January and an appraisal mission in April 1992. On the basis of those investigations, the project staff prepared an appraisal report for the Bank's Board, who formally approved the Project in August 1992. The final step in project approval required the signing of the loan documents by the Bank and the Venezuelan government.

---

[156]Pedro Miguel Reyes, "Judicial Reform in Venezuela" in *Judicial Reform in Latin America*, *supra* note 13, at 166.

[157]Pedro Miguel Reyes, *Venezuela y su experiencia en los programas de reforma judicial* (Paper delivered at the World Bank Conference on Judicial Reform in Latin America and the Caribbean, Washington, D. C., June 13-14, 1994), at 7-8.

2. The Project and the 1992–94 Crisis

After the approval by the Bank's Board, the Project stalled in the chaos generated by the economic and political tumult. The first problem arose with the effort to obtain formal congressional authorization for the government to borrow the US$30 million from the Bank. Under Venezuelan law, all government borrowing for each five-year constitutional period (the Pérez period was to end February 1994) must be approved by the Congress, and capital expenditures and borrowing authorizations are in practice included in an "umbrella" bill. Approval of the umbrella borrowing bill was delayed by the crisis throughout 1992 and early 1993. It was finally approved in March 1993; the final step was the execution of the loan documents by Venezuela before December 31, 1993.

When Pérez was ousted from office in May 1993, though, all of the government ministers involved in the development of the Project were replaced by the interim president, Ramón Velázquez. Thus, the Bank found itself in the position of re-presenting the Project to a new government, whose Minister of Finance, Carlos Rafael Silva, did not believe that the government should borrow for "non-productive" investments during a period of financial crisis.[158] In addition, Rafael Caldera, elected president in December 1993 and scheduled to take office in February 1994, was a staunch opponent of Bank involvement in Venezuelan economic policy. Judicial Council President Pedro Miguel Reyes, a strong supporter of judicial reform, attempted to persuade Velázquez to sign the accord while Finance Minister Silva argued against entering into the loan. This conflict was only resolved at the very last moment, on December 31, 1993, when Caldera's indication of support for

---

[158]Interview with Pedro Miguel Reyes, Caracas, May 1995.

the Project persuaded Velázquez to order the Venezuelan ambassador in Washington to execute the loan documents.[159]

Approval of the loan documents and an indication of support from President Caldera were not enough to get the Project off the ground in 1994. The Bank had to wait for the President and the new Congress to agree on and appoint a new Judicial Council and replace five members of the Supreme Court, and then re-educate both bodies about the Project after the new appointments were in place.[160] However, the collapse of the Venezuelan private banking sector at the outset of 1994 plunged the new Caldera government immediately into crisis and the appointments to the Judicial Council and the Supreme Court magistrates did not occur until September.

C. Venezuelan Reform Proposals During the Crisis

While the Project effectively went on hold during the two most difficult years of the crisis, 1992-94, judicial reform became part of the rallying cry of individuals and political groups proposing an overhaul of the Constitution as a solution to the political tumult.[161]

---

[159]Pedro Miguel Reyes told us that he was assured that the Project documents would be signed only when, after a long day of negotiations at the Presidential palace, he heard a fax machine transmitting the signature authorization to Venezuela's ambassador in Washington as he left to join a New Year's Eve celebration with the president.

[160]Neither the Judicial Council nor the Supreme Court has a professional career staff in place which could serve as an "institutional memory" and source of continuity for administrative projects which continue across presidential administrations. Thus, each new Judicial Council and Supreme Court president must learn about the organization he or she leads on the job; predecessors may have left with key records and the notion of a "transition" process between administrations does not exist.

[161]The President of the Judicial Council later conceded that the reform project "was virtually paralyzed [in 1994], having lost the first year of its useful life." Judicial Council, *Memoria y Cuenta 1994*, at 5.

The Struggle for Reform

President Pérez had reacted to the coup attempt in February 1992 by forming a blue-ribbon committee to develop proposals for reform which would address the decay in the state structure and operation made evident in the wake of the military uprising and the widespread sympathy for the rebels' goal to overthrow a corrupt government. This body proposed the convening of a Constituent Assembly (*Asamblea Constituyente*) (the equivalent of a constitutional convention) to overhaul the Constitution.

Meanwhile, the Congress insisted on pursuing constitutional reform through the legislative process, promising widespread consultations with all social and political sectors. The Chamber of Deputies completed the drafting of the Project for the General Reform of the Constitution at the end of July 1992. The reform bill proposed major changes to the structure of the government, most significantly, handing the executive power over to a new position of Prime Minister. It also proposed changes to the judiciary to remove political influence in the selection of Supreme Court magistrates and lower court judges and to create an independent supervisory and disciplinary commission and a Public Defender charged with the duty of enforcing the civil and political rights of citizens against the state. Thus, constitutional reform shifted from a necessary prelude for the administrative modernization of the state to an imperative destined to save the country from the political crisis generated by the military rebellion.

The utilization of constitutional reform as a mechanism to save the Venezuelan democracy eventually stalled in late 1992. The "consultations" with different social actors clashed with the political interests represented in the Congress who were disposed to accede to every measure except those that would mean the loss of their own privileges. Public opinion surveys revealed that citizens felt defrauded by the consultation process, which appeared motivated more by fear than the necessity for particular constitutional changes. Facing increasing public disenchantment, the Congress decided in October to defer the debate and the reform process for a more auspicious moment. The heated clashes between the supporters of each approach to constitutional revision were cut off for good by the November 1992 coup attempt.

Halfway to Reform

All pending legislation died when the constitutional term ended in February 1994. Therefore, the constitutional reform bill had to be re-introduced and reconsidered by both chambers of Congress. It was formally introduced in the Senate in July 1994; however, almost no action has been taken. In May 1995, Luis Enrique Oberto, President of the Legislative Commission of the Congress, conceded that little congressional interest remained and the constitutional reform bill was, consequently, on indefinite hold.[162] Nonetheless, congressional subcommittees have worked periodically on constitutional and judiciary reform issues in the 1996 Congress. Among the reform options under study is the elimination of the Judicial Council and the transfer of all administrative responsibility for the courts to the Supreme Court.

---

[162]Luis Enrique Oberto, "¿Que Pasa Con La Reforma Constitutional?" *El Nacional*, May 3, 1995.

V. Evaluation Of The Bank's Role

Although Venezuela was the Bank's first free-standing judicial reform project, it has since responded to requests for assistance in this area from other governments in Latin America, Eastern Europe and Asia. With extensive technical resources and experience in public sector restructuring, grants for judicial sector assessments and financing for projects, the Bank has become the most important non-state actor in the field. This role gives the Bank a great degree of influence to affect the shape of reform. The influence derives from the kind of programs it is willing to finance itself and its willingness to insist that a state commit itself to certain reforms as a prerequisite to Bank involvement.[163]

The establishment of the rule of law, enforced by an independent, fair and efficient judiciary is viewed by the Bank a prerequisite for sustained economic growth, social development and democratic consolidation. To build such a judiciary, reform programs should "address the political, economic and legal causes at the root of an inefficient and inequitable judiciary," recognizing that "if such a holistic approach is not adopted, there will be a minimal probability for success."[164]

The basic elements of a reform program should include "measures with respect to guaranteeing judicial independence through changes to judicial budgeting, judicial appointment, and disciplinary systems; improving court administration through the adoption of case management and court management reforms; adopting procedural reforms; providing alternative dispute resolution mechanisms; enhancing the public's access

---

[163]Notwithstanding the influence of the Bank, it is important to reiterate that the responsibility for judicial reform rests with the governments that ask the Bank to provide assistance in this area. We recognize that the Bank is an advisor to governments and do not wish to imply that it is the primary decisionmaker in state reform programs. Rather, we are arguing that the Bank should make certain kinds of recommendations for program design, development and implementation to member states, and only agree to provide assistance when country conditions and government commitment favor reform.

[164]*Elements of Reform*, *supra* note 4, at 7.

to justice . . . and redefining and/or expanding legal education and training programs for students, lawyers and judges."[165]

In evaluating the Bank's performance in Venezuela against this view of reform, concerns are evident in several areas, particularly when assessing the Project in its original form: (i) the development of the Project outside of a comprehensive reform strategy; (ii) the absence of broad government commitment to reform; (iii) the failure of reform strategies to address crucial structural impediments to judicial independence; (iv) the artificiality of economic and non-economic distinctions in key areas of program design; (v) the failure to adequately address access to justice concerns; and (vi) the absence of broad-based participation in the design and development of the Project.

The Project's most serious difficulties grow out of the failure to place the initiative within the context of a comprehensive judicial reform strategy. It developed as a complement to a market-oriented structural adjustment program, focusing on strengthening the management of the Judicial Council when the deeper ills of the judiciary relate to judicial independence issues — the selection and removal of judges, political interference — corruption and access to justice. It failed to obtain broad governmental commitment, relying on the support of a politically-troubled president and a small group of reformers. Few relevant groups outside the government (and few within the judiciary itself) were invited to participate in the Project's design, development or implementation. As a result, the Project was launched with a narrow base of support and almost ended up a casualty of the political crisis that drove President Pérez from office in 1993.

Problems on each of these fronts continue to plague the Project, now four years after Board approval. The government still has no broad reform strategy, the breadth and depth of its interest in substantive reform is unclear, and Judicial Council and Bank promises to expand participation are only slowly being realized.

---

[165] *Id.*

Despite its limited original scope, however, changes have been made in the Project which offer the possibility of enhancing the institutional management and functioning of the courts. And the expansion of the Project during implementation is addressing many of the concerns about the narrowness of the original design and may set the stage for more comprehensive follow-on projects. Those would be important steps forward. Whether they can endure in a judiciary still subject to wide political influence is much less clear. These concerns are examined in greater detail below.

A. Comprehensive Reform

1. The Need for a Long-Term Strategy

The methodological debate over the proper approach to reform involves two issues. First, should a state develop a comprehensive, long-term plan for reform, based on a diagnostic study of the entire judicial sector, before Bank involvement in discreet reform initiatives? And, second, how should reform be sequenced — should constitutional (structural) and legislative measures precede other reforms?

Comprehensive reform. The consensus among those with experience with judicial system reform efforts is that reform should occur within the context of a comprehensive, long-term strategy. The Inter-American Development Bank, for instance, has stated that

> [m]odernization of judicial systems should be viewed as a whole. [A] project that considers only financing of premises or the procurement of computer equipment, in a context marked by a lack of judicial independence, obsolete laws, or administrative disarray, will have little impact on the main goal of creating a reliable, effective, streamlined, and accessible judicial system. The different programs undertaken should be based on a comprehensive approach to the problem and should consider — in light of national circumstances and the requests of the

> authorities — the possibility of providing broad and systematic cooperation that could be carried out in several stages.[166]

AID began providing assistance for judicial reform in Latin America in the early 1980s as part of its mandate to promote the strengthening of democracy.[167] In a review of the effectiveness of legal reform programs supported by AID in El Salvador, Guatemala, Costa Rica, Panama and Colombia, the United States General Accounting Office (GAO) concluded that (i) projects launched without commitment from host governments ready for or receptive to change are generally ineffective and wasteful and (ii) addressing technical problems without confronting the political and institutional obstacles to reform is usually not productive.[168] Regarding the latter point, the GAO noted that

> AID projects focused on easier-to-manage technical assistance, such as judicial training seminars and computerized caseload management, rather than working on the institutional, political, and attitudinal changes necessary for fundamental, sustainable reform. Both the former and the current AID judicial reform manager in El Salvador said that the early strategy was not successful, in part, because AID operated under the assumption that technical changes alone could bring about substantive improvements. For example, AID recognized that El Salvador's legal codes were outdated, and it funded a commission to rewrite

---

[166]Inter-American Development Bank, *Modernization of the State* (September 1994), at 19.

[167]AID's mandate is set by the U.S. Congress and, therefore, reflects the foreign policy interests of the U.S., an ever-present source of tension in its international development activities. AID's assistance is aimed at supporting democratic institutions and the development of a particular vision of a liberal civil society. The scope of its work in judicial reform is thus far wider than that of either the World Bank or the Inter-American Development Bank.

[168]U.S. General Accounting Office, *Foreign Assistance: Promoting Judicial Reform to Strengthen Democracies*, GAO/NSIAD-93-149 (September 1993).

> them. AID and the Commission did not, however, sufficiently concentrate on getting the political support necessary to implement the reforms. Ultimately, few codes were actually revised or implemented because of the lack of political commitment.[169]

In the 1995 assessment of its experience in legal reform initiatives, the World Bank's Legal Department concluded that "the long-term nature of legal reform processes requires a sequence of operations in the context of an overall country assistance strategy of the Bank and, more importantly, that of the legal reform of the borrowing member."[170] In a similar vein, the Bank noted that "countries undergoing legal reforms benefit from in-depth assessments or diagnostic analyses and/or studies of their legal systems (both legal and regulatory frameworks and institutional set-ups) prior to implementing legal technical assistance projects. This applies equally to sector specific, partial legal reforms and

---

[169]*Id.*, at 17. AID defended its judicial reform work, arguing that all of its programs had "aimed at inducing structural or institutional change, including the transformation of the attitudes or political premises on which existing systems are based" and that the GAO had overlooked "the ways in which training, technical assistance and new technologies have been used to promote fundamental attitudinal and institutional reorientation." *Id.*, at 33. Noting that its congressional mandate required its involvement in judicial reform in three Central American countries in which legal reform "was not then a high priority," AID went on to state that its earliest programs in the region "should be viewed as experimental and pilot in nature, intended to generate demand and to build a consensus on reform . . . . [T]he program's strategy was to foster commitment, not to wait until it was present." *Id.*, at 34-35. Finally, AID argued that "[g]iven the managerial and organizational chaos in the sector (a source of or contributor to more serious problems like human rights abuses and corruption), this approach necessarily includes technological components such as case tracking and computerized information systems. Often these concrete and discrete items have provided a valuable incentive to reform and generated a climate for change." *Id.*, at 35. AID did not, however, elaborate on the connection between the technical assistance and climate for change.

[170]*Initial Lessons, supra* note 4, at 17.

to comprehensive ones." The Bank noted that where prior diagnostic efforts were not made (for example, in projects in Bulgaria and the Lao People's Republic) "it seems that . . . a prior assessment might have delayed the projects but made them more effective."[171]

Comprehensive reform requires that a government — in conjunction with the broad range of actors in civil society — acknowledge the fundamental impediments to the functioning of the rule of law and the source of failure to protect constitutionally guaranteed economic, political, civil, social and cultural rights. It presupposes a political effort to generate the broad support needed to initiate and sustain serious reform.

But, more importantly, on a political level a comprehensive diagnostic study is an essential first step in obtaining the broad governmental commitment to reform necessary to sustain the resources for judicial reorganization over several years. A genuine reform effort contemplates the involvement of all judicial system actors in order to secure administrative and procedural coordination, and it logically sequences institutional changes and budgetary resources — and financing from international sources — for each reform phase or project.

Incremental reform. Incremental reform refers to discrete judicial reform projects financed by the Bank as stand-alone measures unrelated to other judiciary initiatives or a comprehensive judicial reform strategy. The approach offers the only alternative in a situation where political or other differences within a state block the possibility of obtaining a consensus for broad reform. The question is whether such efforts are worthwhile and sustainable.

Generally, the answer should be no, for all the reasons that make comprehensive planning important. In addition, stand-alone court improvement programs may have several distorting effects on broader reform efforts, mostly as a result of their tendency (as with the original Venezuela design) to focus on the modernization of institutional operations.

---

[171]*Id.*, at 10-11.

First, institutional strengthening initiatives may shift the focus from or substitute for needed long-term structural changes. While Venezuela's badly-decaying judicial institutions require substantial rationalization and modernization, the absence of the credibility, predictability and fairness critical to the rule of law has to do primarily with the lack of independence of the courts, and only secondarily with administrative disorganization. The Venezuela Project was accepted by the 1990 COPRE-based reform group as an *alternative* to the COPRE congressional proposals aimed at strengthening judicial independence that had been ignored by the Congress.[172]

Second, a focus on technological modernization as a panacea for administrative disorganization is, as the Bank has acknowledged, problematic. The effect may just be the opposite if the introduction of sophisticated technology into a typewriter-and-pencil dominated structure has not been previously analyzed in all of its implications and consequences. In reorganizing information management systems, Venezuelan academic Pérez Perdomo notes, "[t]he point to determine is the purpose of the new technology. If the purpose is to improve the monitoring of cases the first task is not to introduce technology but to design the systems which, once automated, are going to produce this efficiency."[173] For example, one of the principal reasons for the slowness in processing criminal cases in Venezuela is the inability of a judge to get

---

[172]In addition, institution-strengthening projects may provide an excuse for governments to avoid addressing structural problems that facilitate political interference in the operation of the courts. A Bank-funded reform project aimed at the administration of the courts may send the wrong signals to states where the judiciary is dominated by the executive. In Peru, for example, the Bank is developing a reform project with the Peruvian government at the same time that President Fujimori is under heavy international criticism for his oppressive anti-terrorism measures that created a secret penal system marked by "faceless" judges, the use of military tribunals to try civilians and due process restrictions. A judicial reform program for Argentina was put on hold in 1995, supposedly due to economic problems in Argentina, although President Menem had faced intense criticism for his blatant manipulation of the judicial system in the early 1990s.

[173]Informe Sobre Venezuela, *supra* note 89, at 562.

an accused from prison to the court for a hearing or trial because the seats on the buses which would transport the prisoner appear to be the subject of a business run by prison guards. Given that court demand for prison transport always exceeds the transport supply, judges typically request the transfer of a much larger number of prisoners than they can see on a given day so that, in fact, the guards will transport at least a few.[174] A prisoner who does not appear on the day summoned may end up never summoned again. Administrative changes must address these forms of bottlenecks, which can only be resolved on a trans-institutional basis, before technology will make a difference.

These difficulties are not limited to the administrative entities of the judicial system itself. For example, one of the principal reasons why land conflicts take an extraordinary amount of time to resolve — and absorb a considerable amount of a rural court's resources — has little to do with the legal system. The problem lies with the National Agrarian Institute, which has no credible title registry for the parcels of land distributed by the government pursuant to agrarian reform programs. Thus, the courts must endure lengthy and costly battles over title issues about which they cannot obtain reliable information.

A related point — one particularly applicable to Venezuela today — is the fact that the use of computer technology brings with it not only substantial new investments in hardware and software but also ongoing maintenance and training costs and the purchase of specialized personal and office devices for computer usage. The introduction of these new costs at a time when the Judicial Council cannot even provide paper and pens to a deeply underpaid staff could end up paralyzing services.[175] Budgeting and allocating for these costs long after the Bank has left requires the full commitment of the executive and legislative branches. That commitment has not been demonstrated.[176]

---

[174]*Id.*, at 563.

[175]This was an issue raised by several of the individuals with whom we spoke, including the president of the Supreme Court.

[176]*See* discussion below at 102-103.

Third, the bottleneck issue highlights the need for coordination across all of the judiciary agencies often absent from a project that focuses on just a single entity. No reform project — even one with the aims of administrative reorganization and judicial training — will succeed unless officials, both judiciary and non-judiciary, who the system relies upon agree to modify administrative procedures in order to conform to the requirements of a reorganized court system. It is not clear, for example, how the computerization of case management procedures will function if prosecutors, police and prisons do not have access to the same information systems. Nor is it clear how smaller matters affecting the efficient — and fair — functioning of justice, such as the transportation of prisoners and title registry examples discussed earlier, can be resolved without the prior identification of these forms of bottlenecks and a commitment on the part of relevant officials to change. Furthermore, important participants in court proceedings — public defenders and public prosecutors — are not under the jurisdiction of the Judicial Council.[177]

Finally, an incremental initiative such as the Venezuela Project often lacks the base of support within the branches of government, political parties and civil society to guarantee the long-run viability of the project's reforms. In addition, the project's improvements, however meritorious, may well be short-lived if the courts remain heavily influenced by political and private economic interests. The purpose of a comprehensive plan is to generate a broad-based community with a stake in the success of each phase of reform and the commitment to remove the political and economic influences in the courts adverse to change.

Where to begin — from above or below? One of the arguments for incremental reform is based on the assumption that judicial independence is ultimately a characteristic of the way judges act, that is, of judicial

---

[177]Prosecutors within the Public Ministry and the ombudsmen for minors are technically under the jurisdiction of the Public Ministry, while other types of public defenders are the responsibility of the executive. Nevertheless, the reorganization of public defender court offices is included in the Project. *See* discussion above at 45-46.

character and culture, not the result of constitutional or legislative norms designed to provide greater institutional distance between the judicial system and political influence.[178] Transparent selection and appointment procedures, lifetime tenure, guaranteed compensation and retirement benefits and stable financing for the judiciary, in this view, will have little effect unless the judges themselves utilize all of the legal resources at their disposal to enforce fully the laws and defend themselves against political pressure.

The argument asserts that judges are often the most conservative element of a judicial system and likely to be initial opponents of reform initiatives. Thus, the primary task of a judge-oriented strategy is to persuade a "critical mass" of judges of the necessity for reform and to empower this group to carry on the reform process within the judiciary itself. This "reform" core of judges will theoretically serve as the beginning point for the long-term transformation of the judicial culture from one subservient to political and economic influence to one in which the integrity and autonomy of the judicial branch is vigorously defended, regardless of the presence or absence of constitutional or legislative reforms "from above."

This strategy implies a reform sequencing in which the initial phase is focused solely on the consolidation of judiciary support for short-term management and administrative modernization and longer-term institutional reform. Once judicial commitment is achieved, the reform process can expand to address problems in other judiciary institutions and to contemplate broader legislative and constitutional changes.

While the assumptions about the importance of judge-focused efforts are reasonable, the reform sequencing implications that follow conflict with broader reform principles. Most problematically, the need to deal with the judges prior to any reform proposals imposed from "above" (to avoid judicial rejection) suggests that broad-based discussions to identify local needs and priorities and the development of a government-led comprehensive strategy should not occur until after a judge-based project

---

[178] *See Elements of Reform*, *supra* note 4, at 20.

is well under way. This approach contradicts the Bank's own insistence on the necessity for broad government commitment prior to the initiation of a reform plan involving the entire judicial system, supported with input from the government, the legal community and relevant representatives of civil society.

It also de-emphasizes the importance of structural and legislative changes to remove organizational and legal barriers to the effective functioning of reform-minded judges. The formation of a judicial culture in which independence and integrity are primary values can be thwarted by an executive with the ability to remove or demote individual judges or expand the size of a court with "friendly" appointments. The rule of law can be subverted by executives with broad emergency powers whose decrees are, in practice, effectively beyond judicial review.[179] Laws establishing "faceless" courts, for example, or grants of broad jurisdiction over certain kinds of offenses to military courts restrict due process and promote impunity for government abuses, which also undermine public confidence in the judicial system more generally. Constitutional and legislative changes are necessary to remove these impediments to judicial defense of the rule of law.

More fundamental, however, is the concern that — regardless of how vitally it is needed — the strategy to develop a core of reform judges has limitations. First, it is not clear as a sociological phenomena how a small group of judges changes a judicial "culture," particularly when there may exist a large gap in capabilities and motivation between the small reform group and the remaining judges. This is not to say that such leadership is not critical for reform, but rather to emphasize the need for institutional structures to support the vast majority of judges of ordinary character and legal ability who populate any legal system, particularly with a novel (and thus experimental) approach to reform.

---

[179]Venezuela's constitutional economic guarantees, for example, were suspended by presidential decree for most of the 35 years of democratic government. They were restored by Carlos Andrés Pérez in 1990, only to be suspended again by Rafael Caldera in 1994-95.

The Bank seems to have recognized these concerns. Noting that "[j]udicial reform programs based on enhancing the independence of the courts may be politically unfeasible among some members of the legislatures; executive and even the judiciary given the various vested interests," the Bank concludes that "[n]evertheless, independence at the highest levels should be addressed simultaneously."[180]

2. *Venezuela: Incremental and Judge-Oriented*

Despite the clamor for constitutional and judicial reform during the negotiation stages of the Project, no effort was made to develop a long-range reform strategy in Venezuela. In fact, given the reaction of the Venezuelan Congress and political parties to reform proposals in the 1989-92 period, it seemed clear from the beginning of the Bank's involvement that broad reform would not be possible.

The request to the Bank for assistance in judicial reform effectively grew out the conclusion by COPRE and members of the Judicial Council that constitutional and legislative proposals to overhaul outdated legal codes, rationalize the laws governing the judicial sector and reduce political influence in the selection of judges would not get a hearing in Congress.[181] These reform measures had been bottled up in the Congress since 1990 and only the February 1992 coup attempt brought the Congress to return to the issue of reform as a way to escape the political crisis caused by the military rising.[182] The enthusiasm for constitutional

---

[180]*Elements of Reform, supra* note 4, at 20.

[181]The Bank noted in its 1992 Staff Appraisal Report that COPRE had led Venezuelan reform efforts by producing legislative proposals to reduce political influence in the courts by changing appointment procedures and extending the length of judicial terms. The Congress had been considering, at that time, a number of proposals for constitutional (and judicial) reform in light of the February 1992 coup attempt. Venezuela Staff Appraisal Report, *supra* note 38, at 4.

[182]*See* 86-87 above, for a discussion of these events.

reform in the Congress had abated by October 1992, when the several reform proposals before the country — COPRE's package, a group of congressional reforms and the Constituent Constitutional Assembly — were effectively dead. The inability of the Congress and party leaders to agree on a reform proposal in the midst of Venezuela's greatest modern political crisis was an indication of the degree of resistance to the kind of comprehensive reform required for the judicial system.

As an alternative approach, the Bank might have looked for the adoption of the COPRE judicial reform committee's package of bills and the involvement of the Supreme Court, the Ministry of Justice and the Fiscalía General in any reform process as evidence of the broad commitment to reform which would make a Bank contribution worthwhile. In fact, COPRE had argued for these two points. The Bank might also have undertaken a broader diagnostic study — COPRE had already completed a great deal of work in this area — and the development of a long-range reform plan. The Bank, however, settled for a narrow project focus, which ended up precluding the involvement of the Ministry of Justice, the Supreme Court or the Fiscalía, and avoided addressing the need for legislative changes.

The Project ended up adopting (if not developing) the judge-first strategy as early work revealed a need to move beyond judiciary infrastructure improvements and focus on the manner in which judges perform their work. Consequently, neither the Bank nor the Judicial Council desired much exposure for the project (even within the judiciary) until the development of management reforms and a core of reform judges were well under way. As a result, the project seems to have survived (barely) the 1992-94 economic and political crises, but with no broad support or consensus on the direction reform should take. The Bank and the Judicial Council have not yet developed that consensus and the broad government commitment needed to anchor the changes achieved to date in a long-term plan.

B. Government Commitment

In order for legal technical assistance to bring about the desired results, recipient governments "need to establish law reform agendas and prioritize areas where legal assistance is most needed."[183] This notion of government "ownership" of the reform process is critical to its long-term success, as the broad-based institutional changes (across all governmental branches) and elimination of entrenched economic and political power required by legal reform are certain to generate political resistance. As the Bank concedes, "[u]nless a country is committed to reforming its legal regime . . . legal technical assistance may be a waste of resources."[184]

Government commitment should be assessed before the Bank agrees to finance a judicial reform proposal. This assessment should be one of the most important issues in the Bank's initial appraisal of the climate for reform in a given state. Judicial independence is the most important measure of commitment — the willingness of the government to take concrete steps to reduce political influence in judicial appointments and court operations and to dedicate the resources necessary for attracting and training high-caliber judicial candidates.

No such commitment was ever requested of the Venezuelan government. In fact, as noted earlier, the Congress had demonstrated no enthusiasm for legal reform, refusing to address the legislative changes proposed by COPRE between 1987 and 1991. The Project began without the clear commitment of even a majority of the judges whose willingness to accept the proposed changes is critical to the Project's success, gambling that the Judicial Council could persuade most of the courts of the efficacy of the changes as the Project progressed and model courtrooms came on line. It assumed that a successful Project would generate a commitment to further reform on the part of the judiciary and serve as an example to the legislative and executive that reform projects could, in fact, work.

---

[183]*Initial Lessons, supra* note 4, at 11.

[184]*Id.*, at 18.

Evaluation of the Bank's Role

While the commitment of the Pérez administration may have been enough for the Bank to go forward with the Project in 1990 and 1991, the value of that commitment evaporated with Pérez' ouster on corruption charges in May 1993. By the middle of 1993, not a single government minister involved in the development of the Project remained in office; throughout the last half of the year, the Project's supporters had to fight desperately to keep Interim President Velázquez' Finance Minister from withdrawing from the project. And although it was President-elect Caldera's nod which saved the project in the last hours of 1993, Caldera was widely known as a staunch opponent of the Bank's economic adjustment programs.

Entering 1994, therefore, the Bank had almost no official base of support for the Project. In addition, four new members of the Supreme Court and a new Judicial Council were to be appointed by the new president.

Having just witnessed the most severe political crisis in modern Venezuelan history, the Bank ought to have been deeply concerned about the political viability of the Project early on and certainly at the beginning of 1994. Rather than reappraise the climate for reform and the character of the Project given the dramatic changes in the political and economic landscape since the Project was first conceived, the Bank decided to wait on the new appointments and then go forward. Once again, no effort was made to discuss the possibilities for broader reform with the new government. Nor were efforts made to expand judicial sector or civil society participation. Indeed, the near-invisibility of the Project to judges, the Congress and the political parties was characterized by a magistrate close to the Project as a survival strategy — the silence surrounding the reform initiative was needed to give the project time to establish an strong administrative foundation without generating opposition from within the judiciary or the political sector.[185]

Commitment must be demonstrated by actions broader than the establishment of a Private Sector Advisory Group to set the agenda for

---

[185]Interview with member of the Judicial Council, Caracas, May 1995.

reform, as the Bank requested in Ghana, or the creation of a broad-based steering committee to guide consultants carrying out diagnostic studies, as occurred in Argentina.[186] The Bank seems to be moving closer to the mark in some more recent reform work. In Bolivia, for example, where partisan interference was identified as a long-standing problem, the Bolivian Congress approved measures requiring a two-thirds majority of the Senate to appoint Supreme Court members, dedicating three percent of the national budget to the judiciary and requiring a newly-formed judicial council to prepare lists for the appointment of all judges below the Supreme Court.[187] These measures were adopted *prior* to Bank involvement. While the more difficult task of institutionalizing these changes remains, a commitment to get at the root of judicial arbitrariness and ineffectiveness seems to have been made.

C. Judicial Independence

Our analysis of the state of the Venezuelan courts in Chapter II indicated that the most serious problems — arbitrariness, corruption, delays — grow out of the lack of institutional independence of the judicial sector. The lack of an independent judiciary in Venezuela is closely tied to a legal culture in which the state — particularly the executive — historically marginalized and politicized the courts. As a result, respect for legal rules and the integrity of the judiciary fell with each new instance of political interference in the selection of judges and the outcome of controversial cases and with each new revelation of judicial corruption. The judiciary found itself plagued by an "institutional culture" in which legal mandates are simply ignored by the agencies charged by the Constitution or legislation with carrying them out.

The most telling example of this culture is the life of the Judicial Career Law, adopted by the Congress in 1980, which required that all judges be selected by open, competitive examinations. That mandate was

---

[186]*See Initial Lessons, supra* note 4, at 18-19.

[187]Bolivia Staff Appraisal Report, *supra* note 32, at 4-5.

not implemented until 1991. After two such exams, however, the *concurso* was again suspended, this time until 1994. Thus, the exceptional — the temporary appointment of judges — became the norm.[188] As COPRE Executive Director Julio César Fernández Toro notes,

> [t]his occurs with many norms in all areas of the Venezuelan judicial order. A substantial abyss exists between the written law and the actual behavior of the institutional actors obligated to obey it. This culture of disrespect towards written norms, this violation of the principle of the rule of law is the fundamental problem to resolve.[189]

As noted earlier, the Bank fully agrees that judicial independence is the critical issue in most Latin American states, and certainly in Venezuela. Judicial independence "signifies much more than a judge's freedom from political influence," that it includes "structural, organizational and administrative aspects of a judicial system" that range from the method of judicial selection to compensation.[190]

While none of these elements has yet been addressed in the Venezuela Project (except, perhaps, through a study of judicial compensation), the appointment and removal of judges was addressed in the 1994 Ecuador Judicial Sector Assessment[191] and judicial autonomy

---

[188]*See El Nombramiento y Control de Magistrados, supra* note 90, at 14.

[189]*Id.*, at 15-16. Latin America is not the only place where the gap between written law and actual practice is large. The conclusions of a study on Central and Eastern Europe noted that "[l]aws by themselves are only paper; the legal framework will 'come to life' only when the legal and administrative institutions can enforce the laws and readily resolve the disputes they inevitably spur, and when the public accepts that the laws are indeed binding." Cheryl W. Gray, *Evolving Legal Frameworks for Private Sector Development in Central and Eastern Europe*, Discussion Paper No. 209 (World Bank, 1993), at 15.

[190]*Elements of Reform, supra* note 4, at 7-8.

[191]Ecuador Judicial Sector Assessment, *supra* note 31, at 4,16-20.

was discussed in the 1995 staff appraisal report for the Bolivia Judicial Reform Project.[192] In both cases, the governments have initiated constitutional and legislative efforts prior to and in conjunction with the proposed projects aimed at strengthening judicial independence. And in both cases the governments have attempted to develop a long-term comprehensive strategy.

This expansion of Bank consideration of judicial independence issues is a positive step. The Bolivia and Ecuador examples demonstrate that the Bank need not involve itself directly in helping a state to reorganize the way it selects, trains, supervises, compensates and removes judges as long as the issue of institutional independence is included in the initial and continuing discussions among the actors involved in reform and the government takes significant steps to strengthen the judiciary at the outset. And if a government cannot initiate policies to free its judiciary from political influence, the Bank may well conclude that an investment in reform would end up as a waste of resources.

D. The Bank's "Economic" Focus

The Bank's institutional mission to support economic development tends to result in judicial reform program designs which stress artificial distinctions between what are deemed economic and non-economic elements of judicial systems. There is a Bank proclivity to work on commercial codes and civil procedures but to avoid penal issues and procedures and judicial entities that may protect constitutional rights generally but are not seen to have "direct" relevance for commerce or investment. In assessing needs and priorities for judicial reform, the Bank often focuses on a narrowly-defined set of economic actors.

Part of this discrete focus grows out of the Bank's concern about remaining within the scope of its charter mandate and part from the assumption that what investors and merchants primarily seek from judicial systems. To date, there is little research or empirical evidence

---

[192]Bolivia Staff Appraisal Report, *supra* note 32, at 4-5.

documenting the link between the performance of courts and economic development. The available evidence suggests that *political predictability* is probably the more important variable in attracting investment. Political predictability refers to the ability of a political system to establish a set of policies and regulations in an ordered way and to ensure that they are carried out without abrupt change or significant modification. Investors can then rely on the continuance of the set of business rules which led them to the country in the first place.[193]

This kind of political predictability, of course, is attainable in state- as well as market-directed economies, particularly in the short-run. It can be imposed by authoritarian as well as democratic governments. Pinochet's Chile, Singapore, Taiwan, South Korea and China are examples of states that have combined authoritarian politics (repressing human rights, often brutally) and market-oriented growth strategies. Authoritarian governments have been ideally situated to promise stable monetary and fiscal politics, direct investment incentives, a docile labor force[194] and expeditious (although not always impartial) dispute settlement.[195]

Venezuela seemed to bear out this view in 1990-91. The macroeconomic restructuring policies adopted by Carlos Andrés Pérez in 1989 under stringent agreements with the Bank and the IMF generated a tremendous level of new investment in 1990-91 even though the

[193]*See* Beatrice Weder, "Legal Systems and Economic Performance: The Empirical Evidence," *Judicial Reform in Latin America, supra* note 13, at 21-25.

[194]*But see* Arup Banerji and Hafez Ghanem, *Political Regimes, Trade and Labor Policies in Developing Countries*, Policy Research Working Paper No. 1521 (World Bank, October 1995) (suggesting that authoritarian systems that repress labor are more likely than democratic systems to adopt inefficient labor policies inimical to development).

[195]Large investors, in any case, usually contractually provide for dispute resolution in jurisdictions in whose courts they have confidence — usually a United States or European state — and are more concerned about general business conditions and the government's commitment to maintain a favorable macroeconomic business environment.

Venezuelan judiciary was almost universally viewed as highly politicized, inefficient and corrupt. With positive macroeconomic policies creating a favorable economic regime,[196] the condition of the judiciary seemed to play only a minor role in investment decisions.

Moreover, the concerns expressed by foreign and domestic investors about the reliability of the judicial system appear to be a subset of a much broader concern about "judicial insecurity" arising from the fear that fundamental civil and political rights — the right to be free from arbitrary arrest and imprisonment, the right to fair pretrial and trial procedures, the right to be free of unconstitutional actions taken by the government — cannot be vindicated by a deeply politicized and corrupt judiciary. In a 1994 example of this concern, Bruce Haddad, President of the recently-privatized Venezuelan national telephone company, CANTV, was subjected to a *criminal* arrest order in a labor dispute with CANTV employees. With private parties able to file criminal claims in Venezuela, any commercial dispute can be converted into a criminal action. The use of the courts for these kinds of private political ends — known as "judicial terrorism" in Venezuela — may, in fact, affect the climate for investment at least as much as the reliability of courts to resolve commercial disputes.

Economic issues are also implicated in the ability of many Latin American presidents to declare emergencies and rule by decree or through the authority of broad emergency legislation without effective judicial oversight. This practice has played a role in recent Venezuelan history.[197] President Caldera used emergency powers in the recent banking crisis to suspend economic and political guarantees and carry out not only widespread searches and property seizures of those suspected of involvement in the banking sector collapse but also sweeps of crime-

---

[196]At least in the very short run. Most of the inflow was portfolio investment in the Caracas stock exchange rather than direct foreign investment in factories and services. The difference is that the former can be withdrawn from the country on a moment's notice — which occurred in 1992 as the coup attempts undermined political stability.

[197]See the discussion of Carlos Andrés Pérez' suspension of constitutional guarantees above at 70-71.

ridden poor neighborhoods, actions having nothing to do with the banking crisis.[198] But they do suggest that neither human rights nor economic reforms nor investments are secure if an executive can so easily and arbitrarily change a government's course.

Therefore, the scope of judicial reform from the perspective of the Bank's own mandate should encompass all elements that will strengthen the court's ability to hold the other branches within the bounds of the constitution and laws of a state, thus providing the broad sense of judicial security necessary for economic and social development. Whether those elements include rural land courts and land title procedures,[199] coordinating civil and criminal procedure to avoid administrative bottlenecks[200] or assisting the Public Prosecutor to strengthen a human rights unit,[201] they should be included in reform plans (whether or not they are part of a Bank-supported project) where they reflect local needs and priorities. The Bank's Ecuador Judicial Sector Assessment, for example, called for general improvements in criminal procedure laws, noting problems like prolonged prison detention "contribute[] to the loss of confidence by the public in the impartiality and unfairness of the legal system. Since the criminal law affects the general population directly, it

---

[198]*See* discussion above at 71-72.

[199]*See* discussion above at 96. In the Ecuador Judicial Reform Project, the Bank is financing a preparatory study for modernization of Ecuador's property registry system. *See* Ecuador Staff Appraisal Report, *supra* note 52, at 97-100.

[200]*See* discussion above at 96.

[201]Efforts to support the Public Prosecutor's responsibilities to enforce the Venezuelan Constitution's human rights guarantees (which include as incorporated into Venezuelan law the human rights guarantees contained in the International Covenants and the American Convention) provide a highly effective way to enforce the rule of law and assure the protection of economic, as well as civil, political, social and cultural rights. Human rights norms enjoy the same legal status as all other constitutional, commercial or penal norms in Venezuela.

has a profound affect on the public's perception of the entire system."[202]

E. Access to Justice

The ability of those with fewer resources to use the courts is a key measurement of the functioning of a judicial system. Access is critical for small business persons attempting to enforce contracts or defend intellectual property as well as individuals attempting to vindicate human rights guarantees. In fact, access to justice is an area that implicates the Bank's "overarching objective" of poverty alleviation:

> The legal framework also affects the lives of the poor and, as such, has become an important dimension of strategies for poverty alleviation. In the struggle against discrimination, in the protection of the socially weak, and in the distribution of opportunities in society, the law can make an important contribution to an equitable and just society and thus to prospects for social development and poverty alleviation. Conversely, the legal framework can cement existing inequalities through laws that discriminate by race, religion, ethnic affiliation, national origin, or sex, or where tax laws, land laws, family laws, and social security laws fail to protect the weak or discriminate against them. Inherent in the concept of the rule of law is the notion of fairness and social justice.[203]

---

[202]Ecuador Judicial Sector Assessment, *supra* note 31, at 33. The same point is made in a 1993 World Bank report on Viet Nam: "Confidence in the legal system as a whole is necessary to support new economic behavior, so that new laws and regulations are required not just in the economic sphere but in all areas in which individuals, enterprises, and government agencies rely on the legal system to protect their rights and define their obligations." World Bank, *Viet Nam, Transition to Market, An Economic Report*, Report No. 11902-VN (September 15, 1993), at 41.

[203]*Governance, supra* note 18, at 23.

The Venezuela Project does not include an access-to-justice component, even though, as described above, the courts are out-of-reach for most of the Venezuelan population.[204] In a more recent judicial reform initiative, the Bank has recognized the importance of reforms that instill broad public confidence in and provide for popular access to the courts. The Ecuador judicial sector assessment, for example, argued that Ecuador should "establish legal services that make the system as accessible as the Constitution intends. The justice system is for the entire population and there should not be additional barriers for the poor in order to use the system. Accordingly, the system of public defenders should be revised and the number of public defenders should be increased so that they may satisfy their mandate. In addition, legal aid should be established throughout the country . . . ."[205] The Ecuador Judicial Reform Project that was approved by the Bank's Board contains access to justice components, including support for a pilot program to provide legal services to indigent women.[206]

F. Participation

Although long criticized for failure to include non-governmental "consumers" in the design and implementation of economic development projects, the Bank has in recent years moved to increase the "participation" of a broader array of "stakeholders" in the projects it funds, recognizing that "[t]here is significant evidence that participation can, in many circumstances, improve the quality, effectiveness and

---

[204]*See* discussion above at 63-67. The Project does, however, include authorization for a study on access to justice by the poor.

[205]Ecuador Judicial Sector Assessment, *supra* note 31, at 27.

[206]Ecuador Staff Appraisal Report, *supra* note 52, at 73-83, 97-100. No access to justice components are included in the Bolivia or Russian Federation projects.

sustainability of projects, and strengthen ownership and commitment of government and stakeholders."[207]

In the area of legal reform, the Bank states that "[w]hen designing strategy for assistance, it is important to receive as much input and advice as possible not only from the partner governments but also from local bar associations, legal research institutes, law school faculties, judiciary, chambers of commerce, parliaments, individual lawyers and the public."[208] More importantly, the Bank recognizes that "[t]o have an impact on the

---

[207]World Bank, *The World Bank and Participation* (September 1994), at i. This report was produced by the Bank-wide Learning Group on Participatory Development launched in December 1990 with the task of identifying challenges to the Bank in "stepping up" its efforts to support participation in its operations. The definition of "stakeholder" remains vague. For the Bank, "[r]elevant stakeholders are determined by the situation and type of activity to be supported. Not all parties with an interest can be automatically assumed to be relevant. . . . Key stakeholders are clearly those intended to be directly affected by a proposed intervention, *i.e.*, those who may be expected to benefit or lose from Bank-supported operations; or who warrant redress from any negative effects of such operations, particularly among the poor and marginalized. Those indirectly involved or affected can include persons or institutions with (i) technical expertise and public interest in Bank-supported policies and programs; and (ii) linkages to the poor and marginalized. Such stakeholders may include NGOs, various intermediary or representative organizations, private sector business and technical and professional bodies." *Id.*, at 2. The Bank goes on to caution, though, that "meaningful and broad-based participation is not easily achievable and is not without costs or risks. However, the evidence collected shows that, more often than not, the benefits of participation outweigh the costs . . . though this is not always easy to quantify." *Id.*, at 5. Nevertheless, the Bank notes that its charter prohibits it from viewing participation as an end in itself related to democratization or other political values: "Given the Bank's focus on economic development, its interest in participation is primarily one of improving the results of its investments." *Id.*, at 19.

[208]*Initial Lessons, supra* note 4, at 22.

society at large, legal reform cannot be achieved exclusively by the legal profession; it should involve a broader audience."[209]

The form participation actually takes is not as important as the fact that it take place early and provide the opportunity for a broad range of views to be heard. This can be achieved

> through a process of creating a global plan created by the various actors (including the judicial council or similar committee). This action plan has only been tried to date in Ecuador, and it has been successful in planning future reform efforts. Other methods have included holding workshops and town meetings in order to plan a project for reform. This method was employed in Costa Rica where over 6,000 people participated in the design of the Inter-American Development Bank Project. Sector reviews can provide the initial information necessary to begin such discussions with the actors involved and with the government . . . . As a result, a plan can be developed together with the public and private sector. These efforts are important for building the necessary consensus prior to implementing any reform since judicial reform will affect the private sector, the public, the legal community, as well as member of the judiciary.[210]

---

[209]*Id.*, at 23. While stating this principle, representatives of the non-governmental community were noticeably absent from a World Bank-organized meeting to promote the discussion and exchange of ideas on judicial reform in Latin America (*Conference on Judicial Reform in Latin America and the Caribbean*, June 1994, Washington, D.C.). The one NGO from Ecuador that did attend was present on its own initiative and at its own expense. NGOs have also been absent from similar Inter-American Development Bank meetings, for example, the February 1993 *Seminar on Justice in Latin America and the Caribbean in the 1990s* in Costa Rica and the October 1995 *Second Conference on Justice and Development in Latin America and the Caribbean* in Montevideo, Uruguay.

[210]*Elements of Reform*, *supra* note 4, at 68. Often overlooked, but essential for there to be any hope of meaningful participation is language accessibility, *i.e.*, the need for key documents and information to be available in the language of those people the Bank and government seek to involve in development activities.

Participation was not a recognized Bank policy in 1990, when discussions concerning the Venezuelan project began. Not surprisingly, then, Bank discussions were limited to members of the Judicial Council and the Pérez cabinet, with some consultations with COPRE and visits to a few large law firms and a major chamber of commerce. But other major actors in the judicial system — the Ministry of Justice and the Public Prosecutor most prominently — had very little input, and almost no actors in civil society — academia, bar associations, law faculties, NGOs — were contacted.

More surprising is that only a handful of judges were consulted and the vast majority knew little of the contents of the Project other than that which they had read in newspapers as late as May 1995. The President of the Supreme Court, Rafael Alfonso Guzmán, appointed in 1995, told us that the Supreme Court knew very little of the Project as of mid-1995. Magistrate Guzmán recalled a meeting with Bank representatives in March at which the court was briefed on the reform proposal, but he could recall little of its substance. He had recently received a proposal from the Bank for computerizing the Supreme Court, but his initial response was that the court would not have sufficient funds going forward for maintenance and staff training for a new system, and the court had other problems to address first.[211]

To a large extent, the lack of broad consultation in the design phase reflected the Project's rushed development as a companion measure to Venezuela's larger structural adjustment program and the Bank's traditional practice of dealing principally with its "client," the government. It also reflects, however, a view of the participation process growing out of the approach to reform in which the first phase focuses on

---

While there have been some improvements in this area, most Bank documents continue to be available only in English. This is largely an issue of resources — the cost of translation — but needs to be addressed.

[211]Interview with Rafael Alfonzo Guzmán, President of the Supreme Court of Justice, Caracas, May 1995.

bringing judges into the reform process. In principle, this approach calls for broad (but not public) initial consultations to identify judicial system needs and priorities for the design of a plan. A second participation phase involves only the judges, who are consulted and briefed on reform through workshops. After this initial project phase, when the judges have been brought onto the process, a third stage of participation occurs when the broad public is informed and invited to assist in developing and supporting follow-on projects.

As we noted in an earlier discussion, however, this "staged" participation process in practice results in rather limited preliminary consultations (as occurred in Venezuela) and a delay in the development of a comprehensive plan and the necessity for broad government commitment until after a judge-oriented project. And, in fact, the judges are not simply oriented to the *idea* of reform but to a concrete program (usually one to modernize the way the courtrooms and dockets are managed by judges and the judicial system is administered by its organizational authority). Thus, participation tends to mean a process of explaining an already-designed reform plan to and seeking support from the public. And because it initially focuses only on the judges, other judiciary organs are left out.

The failure of the Project to involve other administrative entities threatens more than communication — to the extent that the aims of the Project require the assistance of the Ministry of Justice and the Public Prosecutor in adapting their procedures to those of an administratively reorganized Judicial Council, the failure of participation can have serious repercussions for the long-term effectiveness of the Project itself. And to the extent that each administrative entity continues to jealously guard its prerogatives, the Bank ends up strengthening one arm of the judiciary against the rest, provoking conflict.

Participation attempts to ensure that reform programs are designed to address the right problems, the issues of concern to the "consumers" of the judicial system, not only the interests of the service providers. Participation permits the surfacing of opposition early, at a moment when design is still flexible and can accommodate unanticipated needs or problems. And, perhaps most importantly, participation encourages the development of a broad social base for reform programs, giving the society at large a role in the transformation of its system of justice, a role that may help broad reform projects survive unexpected political and economic crises.

In spite of the expressed willingness of Bank officials and the Judicial Council to begin to reach out to civil society, the Project is only slowly emerging from the cloak of secrecy which has covered it since its inception. The advisory commission, as noted, still is not functioning, although an effort is underway to revive it. Judges are becoming better informed — fully ten percent of the judges have participated in workshops — but many still lack detailed information. Unfortunately, no sustained effort has yet been made to incorporate bar associations, NGOs, the law schools, chambers of commerce or neighborhood associations in the reform process, although the Judicial Council and Bank representatives in Venezuela have recently expressed a strong interest in bringing NGOs and the public generally into the reform process.[212]

G. Coordination of Donor Involvement

Because of its global scope and interdisciplinary expertise, the Bank views itself as well-positioned to act as coordinator of external legal technical assistance in its borrowing member countries. In Latin America, the Inter-American Development Bank and United States and European governments and organizations are also active in financing judicial reform efforts, often supporting projects in countries in which the Bank is also providing technical assistance. Coordination of activities among these entities and the judicial sector is haphazard, depending largely on the interest and ability of project managers at the country level to meet and

[212]World Bank staff met with Provea and the Lawyers Committee in Venezuela and Washington, D.C. on several occasions to discuss the Venezuela Project and judicial reform in general. The Bank also sent a representative to an NGO meeting on judicial reform in Latin America. These discussions have been fruitful, but they do not constitute "participation" *vis-a-vis* the Project as they have not involved the wider non-governmental community in Venezuela.

agree to the particular projects each should finance. More often than not, the coordination that does exist ends after each entity has defined its operational area — the Bank and the IDB working on administrative reform and judicial training and AID addressing prison reform, for example. As the Bank concedes, "in many countries legal technical assistance is being provided from a variety of sources and frequently without proper coordination. This may lead to inconsistent pieces of legislation being drafted or inconsistent institutions being promoted."[213]

In response to this problem, the Bank has suggested that one option for overall coordination of judicial reform is the formation of a separate agency, a legal reform unit (LRU) within the executive branch of a recipient government. To date, LRUs have been formed exclusively in states undergoing comprehensive reform, such as Bulgaria, many republics of the former Soviet Union and Pakistan.[214]

But the haphazardness of reform programs originating from several sources is a consequence of the failure of a state to develop a long term strategy and then to seek technical assistance and financing from the most appropriate source for each project phase. In this situation, the Bank could use its experience in program management to encourage the consistent and complementary design of projects across the judicial sector. In Venezuela, this would currently involve coordination among the Bank, the German Federal Ministry for Economic Cooperation and Development (financing a penal code reform project) and the congressional committees dealing with various reform initiatives.

While the Bank is currently the only international financial entity involved in judicial reform in Venezuela, serious coordination problems exist among the four entities which comprise the judicial sector. Each

---

[213]*Initial Lessons, supra* note 4, at 9.

[214]*Id.*, at 20. While most LRUs have been governmental agencies, the Russian Foundation for Legal Reform, the implementing agency for the Russia Legal Reform Project approved in June 1996, is a quasi-governmental entity founded by government and non-government parties. Russia Technical Annex, *supra* note 33, at 21.

operates independently of the rest and contact, let alone cooperation, among them has been rare. The Bank attempted to address this problem at the outset by establishing a project advisory committee consisting of a representative from each ministry. With nothing directly at stake in the Project, however, interest in the committee diminished and the Bank did not work to keep it together. A LRU in the executive branch does not make much sense in Venezuela's case as long as the executive branch judicial sector agencies have no direct involvement in reform. A more practical suggestion is to revive and expand the oversight and coordination responsibilities of the advisory committee, adding representatives from the Congress and civil society. A longer-run strategy — which might suggest consideration of a LRU — is to develop follow-on programs that would bring reform initiatives to all of these agencies, giving each a stake in the success of the whole.

H. The Project on Its Merits

The Project does address a limited number of the difficulties plaguing the court system. Its broadest focus is on the catastrophic state of judicial administration and court and case management. And in proposing to strengthen the ability of the Judicial Council to actually manage and plan for over 1,000 courts, the Project is laced with management studies that are to precede the development of new administrative procedures and technology systems. At the planning stages, then, the Bank seems to be taking a prudent approach to administrative restructuring, attempting to identify systemic problems and then designing administrative and technology solutions, rather than turning to technology as a panacea *per se*. Our investigation left the overwhelming impression that the level of management and computer sophistication in the courts is strikingly low. Training court personnel in basic administrative office procedures — accounting, record-keeping, contract management, filing, statistical reporting — will have to precede the overlay of automated procedures.

Computerized case management should permit judges, court personnel, lawyers, litigants and the general public to determine the status of pending cases without time-consuming visits to a court archive. At present, litigants must check the official court file on a daily basis to determine if the judge has taken or ordered any action. A computerized record will also eliminate much of the ability of individuals to manipulate cases by removing or "losing" orders filed in the court record. It should also permit the Judicial Council to monitor the workloads and backlogs of each judge on a real-time basis, data never before available to the Council.

A proposed computerized data base on current legislation and jurisprudence — with abstracts of recent Supreme Court decisions — would give users of the legal system timely and uniform access to important juridical norms for the preparation of cases and appeals. It should aid judges and appellate courts to interpret legislative norms more consistently.

The most dramatic change suggested for the courts by the Project is the manner in which individual judges work. Currently, each judge is, in effect, an independent court complete with secretary, bailiff, file clerks, archive, five to fifteen law assistants (usually law students) and public window. The court office is usually very crowded with staff, lawyers and litigants intermingling, with very little privacy for judge or staff. The judge is responsible for all the administrative functions of the court.

The Project has designed several new pilot courtroom models to be tested in a number of different regions. The most innovative (the "multiple judge" model) locates three to ten judges of the same legal jurisdiction in the same physical courthouse. Management is assigned to a chief judge and a court administrator, lifting many of the management duties from the individual judges. Sentencing judges would be separated from the general public. New computerized case management and word processing systems should free additional judicial time for legal matters. Automation should also permit several judges to share a common secretariat, reducing the ratio of judges to support staff by perhaps half and freeing up resources.[215] Because of the dramatic changes it makes in the judge's role — particularly in the loss of independent control of staff

[215]*See* Venezuela Staff Appraisal Report, *supra* note 38, at 9.

and administration — this model is expected to face the most resistance among sitting judges.[216]

The Project may also provide the basis for improved responsiveness from public defenders, who currently share general office space with judges and court personnel and are perceived to be part of the court system rather than independent representatives of their indigent clients.[217] A new "corporate" model creates a separate public defender office in the courthouse for all defenders working in the building. Cases are collected in the office and then evenly distributed to defenders. The public lawyers will share a common office administrator and be expected to establish common defense strategies. The office will also provide direct access and information to the public. The important step is the separation of the defenders from a direct administrative relationship with, and dependence on the judges and the effort to establish an independent public defender "culture."[218]

And the revival of the judicial school is critical for preparation for the judicial career and continuing education for sitting judges. While Venezuela has some excellent jurists, complaints are widespread about the lack of adequate legal training for judges in all judicial matters, the inability or unwillingness to follow written procedures and the failure to follow existing jurisprudence. The Project's objective is modest — to get the school up and running with a basic curriculum in two years. The school administration has responded positively to an offer by Provea to

---

[216]Other models will be tested simultaneously. The "individual judge" model most resembles the existing structure, with each judge maintaining complete autonomy over court administration and staff. Efficiencies would be expected from new computer systems and simplified administrative procedures. Once tested, the models are to be installed in up to 50% of all courtrooms. *Id.*, at 31-33.

[217]*See* discussion above at 63-66.

[218]The Bank will test models which establish public defender offices outside of the courthouse as well as models only marginally different from today's practice.

provide a human rights law training module for the school curriculum; Provea offered the course at the school when it last functioned in 1991.

Finally, the Project provides a basis for follow-on proposals through a series of studies of various issues related to the functioning of the judiciary. The studies address, among other issues, judicial salaries, the impact on the courts of alternative dispute resolution procedures and alternative means to improve access to justice to the poor.[219] As a whole they do not add up to a comprehensive diagnostic analysis; more importantly, they do not reach the issues which determine the ability of the judiciary to function as an independent, non-partisan check on government power and to effective redress human rights violations. They can, however, serve as the basis for a broad dialogue directed at the use of the Project as a "launch pad" for comprehensive reform.

The success of these modest — but significant — proposals, of course, depends upon factors originally avoided by the Bank and the Judicial Council: the depolitization of the courts and the Judicial Council, the weeding out of the corrupting influences of the judicial "tribes," and the political commitment to provide the resources for an independent judicial sector during years of economic crisis.

Encouragingly, movement in this direction has begun. As preliminary work on the Project got underway, it became clear to the Bank and the Judicial Council that the resistance of judges to reform would have to be addressed if administrative changes were to succeed. The Bank then designed a strategy to develop a core of judges committed to the reform process who would take a leadership role on specific reform initiatives within the judiciary. This core was identified and developed through a series of workshops held in the second half of 1995. A judicial commission of 28 judges is now carrying out training and development activities withing the judiciary.

In addition, three other judiciary actors not involved in the Project — the Supreme Court, the Ministry of Justice and the Public Ministry — have expressed an interest in receiving Bank help with judicial reform

---

[219]Venezuela Staff Appraisal Report, *supra* note 38, at 49.

programs of their own. At this writing, the Bank is discussing reform possibilities with the Supreme Court.

Finally, the Bank is conducting an assessment of the project and the long-term needs for judicial reform in Venezuela which may serve as the basis for the development of a truly comprehensive plan.

Conclusions and Recommendations

A. Conclusions

The World Bank has become a major actor in judicial and legal reform efforts in Latin America at a critical juncture in the democratization process now underway in almost all countries in Central and South America. At stake is the ability of the judiciary to check the power of governments and protect the rights of all actors — individuals, groups and other entities — while preserving the state's ability to vindicate legitimate government interests.

Judicial reform is the responsibility of governments — particularly the tasks of developing a consensus on the need for and scope of reform and the design of a long-term reform strategy. The Bank provides advice to governments on reform strategy and offers technical and financial support for discreet reform initiatives. In this critique, the Lawyers Committee and Provea have focused on the content of the Bank's advice and the conditions under which it participates in reform projects while emphasizing that the overall responsibility for reform lies with the states themselves.

Within this context, the Bank's role in the design and implementation of the Venezuela reform project raises a number of serious concerns.

- The Venezuela Project was not designed as a component of a comprehensive long-term reform program. A comprehensive plan means more than identifying the range of problems plaguing a judicial system; its real importance lies in developing and sequencing reform initiatives in a logical progression, eventually including all of the system's actors, each of whose operations affects the ability of the rest to function efficiently and fairly. The development of such a plan is not the responsibility of the Bank but rather the government seeking to improve its judicial system. The Bank can and should, however, insist that reform (including any Bank projects) be based on a long-range strategy that involves all judicial sectors and identifies needed constitutional and legislative changes. That strategy, in turn, should grow out of a detailed judicial sector analysis and broad public consultation. No such plan has been developed in Venezuela even though the need for judicial reform has been a major political issue for several years.

- Since the Project only focused on providing institutional support and infrastructure improvements for the Judicial Council and was not developed in the context of a wider program, the most serious problems in the Venezuelan judiciary — lack of judicial independence from political influence and corruption — were not addressed.
- No broad government commitment to reform was obtained prior to the decision to go forward with the Project. The Bank essentially — and, as it turns out, disastrously — relied upon the support of President Carlos Andrés Pérez for the Project's political viability. It was almost terminated during the waning days of the Velázquez interim presidency. One result of the lack of an executive and congressional consensus on the scope of reform is a fragmented, uncoordinated discussion of reform options among ministries and legislative committees. One proposal now under review would eliminate the Judicial Council, the heart of the existing Project, and give to the Supreme Court the responsibility to administer the appellate and lower courts.
- The scope and content of the Project were negotiated between the Bank, the Judicial Council and the Pérez administration with very limited input from the judicial and legal community and the private sector and no input from NGOs or the general public.
- Participation in the Project remains limited to the judicial sector, in spite of the widespread calls across Venezuelan society for fundamental reform of the court system. The Project has not (yet) served as a catalyst for discussions of broader reform; it has remained largely hidden from public view. The Judicial Council has, however, responded positively to the interest of Provea and the Lawyers Committee in the Project and is discussing ways to open the Project to broader participation.

B. Recommendations to the World Bank

With Regard to Judicial Reform Generally:

In recent publications reviewing its role in judicial reform programs, the Bank has set forth a judicial reform strategy that emphasizes the need for judicial reform to take place within the context of long-term plans incorporating both the structural reforms required to support greater judicial independence and organizational and administrative reforms to improve the day-to-day operations of the courts and the performance of judges. This strategy, which also stresses widespread participation in the development and implementation of reform projects, reflects, in principle, many of the views of the Lawyers Committee and Provea outlined in this report. This document has also demonstrated, however, that most of those Bank principles were not applied to the Venezuela Project. While Bank policy and practice are developing with each new reform project, concerns about similar gaps between Bank policy and practice have been noted by NGOs following judicial reform in other countries. Therefore, the Lawyers Committee and Provea would like to emphasize a number of points applicable to reform efforts generally:

1. In assessing whether to respond to a government's request for judicial reform assistance, the Bank should give highest priority to the demonstration of government commitment to broad reform, particularly if political interference is a serious obstacle to the proper administration of justice. "Demonstrated" commitment should come in the form of concrete measures (such as reforming the way judges are selected) implemented prior to or contemporaneously with a Bank-financed initiative.

2. To help design a reform program that reflects broad social concerns about the judiciary (as well as to guarantee multi-year support for comprehensive reform), the Bank should seek to ensure that all sectors of society have an opportunity to participate in the development of a reform package. This participation should occur from the beginning of the process in accordance with a participation plan. The Bank should

view individuals and organizations in civil society as allies (as well as the Bank's ultimate clients) whose ideas and support can greatly enhance the chances for success of Bank projects in this area.

3. Access to justice problems for all citizens should be addressed in each reform plan and included in Bank components or other initiatives.

With Regard to the Venezuela Project:

1. The Bank and Judicial Council should encourage an expansion of the role of the Project in the judicial reform discussions currently underway in Venezuela, utilizing the Project as the basis for broader follow-on reform initiatives of both an institutional and an administrative nature. The Bank should facilitate this process within the scope of its existing work as follows:

a. Recommend the reactivation of the Project oversight committee with broad policy responsibility for the overall direction of the Project. The oversight committee should continue to include the officials heading the several judicial sector entities (Supreme Court, Judicial Council, Ministry of Justice, Public Ministry, Military Courts) but should be expanded to include representatives from the legislature, COPRE, the legal profession, the bar associations, the lower-court judges, the law schools, and organizations in civil society. The oversight committee might be an appropriate body to coordinate ongoing reform efforts, given its intergovernmental character, and to educate the public on reform issues.

b. Utilize existing funds allocated for studies to broaden the analysis of the judicial system's problems and to develop proposals for follow-on reform projects. A reconstituted oversight committee could supervise the development of new studies, which would most likely look at the functioning of the judicial sector entities not currently the focus of reform activities.

c. Establish a mechanism to coordinate with other multilateral and bilateral entities active in the judicial reform area for assistance with immediate reform needs not addressed by the Project. The most pressing short-term concern is the modernization and reform of criminal procedure and the institutions responsible for assuring that criminal suspects are detained, interrogated, imprisoned and tried fairly — the Ministry of Justice, the PTJ, the Public Prosecutor. Most individual human rights violations occur in connection with police involved in extrajudicial killings, warrantless arrests and torture during interrogation. The courts must dramatically improve their ability to hold police accountable by requiring proper warrants and providing prompt and fair hearings.

2. Immediately develop and implement a participation plan to involve the legal community and civil society in the remaining phases of the Project and any follow-on initiatives.

* * * * *

Recent Project developments have left the Lawyers Committee and Provea guardedly hopeful that the Venezuela initiative is beginning to expand its scope to overcome some of its most serious design limitations. One shift has been to move from working just with the Judicial Council to incorporate the judges (or at least a number of judges) into the reform process. Reportedly, approximately ten percent of Venezuela's judges have participated in reform-oriented workshops and a group of these judges is taking an active role in training work within the judiciary. A second shift has been the expression of interest of other judicial sector actors, particularly the Supreme Court, in obtaining Bank assistance for their own reform projects. A third change has been an expression of interest on behalf of the Judicial Council (and the Bank) in opening up the reform process to the participation of NGOs and other non-judiciary, non-governmental actors. And, finally, it appears that the Bank is undertaking a broad assessment of the Project which might set the stage for broader follow-on reform programs.

These are all positive, if small, steps in the right direction. As this report goes to press, though, not enough information is available to assess the effects of these shifts, nor what (if anything) the Bank or the Judicial Council will recommend in terms of further expansion of the reform program. It remains clear, though, that four years after Executive Board approval of the Project, Venezuela has yet to begin the process of developing a consensus on the scope of judicial reform or to demonstrate broad government commitment to the principle of reform. While procuring consensus and commitment is not the responsibility of the Bank, judicial reform efforts (including the Project) will not succeed in their absence. Getting this process underway is still the major judicial reform challenge in Venezuela today.

APPENDIX A

A Report of the Conference on Judicial Reform in Latin America: The Role of Multilateral Development Banks

June 10-11, 1996
Caracas, Venezuela

In June 1996, the Lawyers Committee for Human Rights and the Venezuelan Program for Human Rights Education and Action (Provea) convened a conference on *Judicial Reform in Latin America: The Role of Multilateral Development Banks* in Caracas, Venezuela. The meeting brought together 21 legally-focused human rights and environmental NGOs from ten countries in South and Central America. Mr. Roberto MacLean represented the World Bank and Ms. Christina Biebesheimer spoke on behalf of the Inter-American Development Bank (IDB). Also participating were representatives of three Venezuelan government bodies — the Judicial Council, the Presidential Commission for the Reform of the State and the Judiciary School. A list of the conference participants follows this report.

The purpose of the meeting was to examine and exchange perspectives on the role of the two banks in judicial and legal reform efforts in several countries in the region. The conference addressed three broad themes: the approach of each bank to judicial reform, NGO views on reform priorities and the participation of NGOs (and civil society generally) in the development and implementation of bank reform projects. The NGOs ended the conference with a workshop on NGO strategies for participation in judicial reform initiatives. Each theme was presented by a panel to the group as a whole and followed by comments and critiques from participants. Several papers were circulated to participants before or at the meeting which provided additional perspectives on the issues discussed.*

---

*Among the papers distributed were: a draft of the Lawyers Committee and Provea paper "Halfway to Reform: The World Bank and the Venezuelan Justice System"; "La Función Social del Juez: La Cultura de Servicio en la Administración de Justicia," by Roberto G. MacLean; "Apontamentos Sobre a

This report is a distillation of the discussions that occurred at the meeting. It was prepared by the Lawyers Committee and Provea and does not purport to represent the views of others who attended the meeting, some of whom may disagree with the following description.

A. The Approach to Judicial Reform

The first day of the conference focused on policy and strategic approaches to judicial reform in light of the problems facing legal systems in Latin America. The policy debates focused on whether MDB-supported reform should 1) emanate from a comprehensive, long-term, country-designed plan or proceed on a project-by-project basis; 2) address structural problems affecting judicial independence and autonomy or focus initially on institutional and administrative support for the development of a judicial "culture" characterized by judges willing to fully and fairly enforce legal norms; and 3) involve broad participation from legal and civil society in the design and implementation of reform proposals. Mr. MacLean and Ms. Biebesheimer provided overviews of the approaches of the World Bank and the IDB, respectively. These presentations were followed by comments from a representative of the Venezuelan government agency at the heart of judicial reform efforts and a Venezuelan NGO. Conference participants then offered their observations.

The World Bank. Mr. MacLean characterized the administration of justice as a service provided by the state to its citizens. The justice system maintains social peace and facilitates economic development by providing an independent and fair tribunal for the settlement of disputes. The ultimate beneficiary of judicial reform, then, is the citizen, not the judge. The goal of judicial reform is to permit the judicial power to provide a better service to citizens and economic actors in society.

(Dis)Função e o (Des)Funcionamento do Judiciario," by T. Miguel Pressburger; "Proyecto de Reforma del Sistema de Administración de Justicia en el Perú y Derechos Humanos," by Roger Niego Arana; "La Protección del Medio Ambiente: Las Acciones de Interés Público," by Carlos Chirinos Arrieta.

In Mr. MacLean's view, the principal obstacle to achieving this goal, and one of the principal problems limiting commerce, investment and development, is the vast gulf in many countries between the written law and the way social and economic rules actually function. The judge is the only actor in society who must face this contradiction every day as an integral part of his or her work. Unfortunately, many judicial systems in the developing world do not function well enough to encourage the judge to bridge the gap between abstract law and reality. Given this failure, Mr. MacLean argued that real reform can only come about by focusing on developing the conscience of judges about their social role. Neither the provision of necessary financial resources nor the gaining of broad political support to modify the constitution or legislation will result in real reform unless a core group of judges develops the dedication, commitment and support to revitalize the judiciary from within. Reform, then, must begin with the judge and the success of any reform initiative will depend upon the extent to which the judges themselves change the way they enforce the law and defend the independence of the judiciary as an institution. Constitutional and legislative changes to strengthen the autonomy and independence of judges will fail unless the judges themselves develop the capacity and institutional culture to act independently of political or economic pressure in the fulfillment of their judicial roles. While changes in laws and systems can effect some improvements, no real or significant change can be achieved if, first, there is not a group of judges to implement the changes.

Mr. MacLean insisted that the World Bank's focus on the role and character of the judge does not mean that the Bank is not interested in long-term comprehensive reform. He stated that the Bank develops its reform recommendations after an evaluation of nine elements in a justice system: the legal context; the administration of the judicial system; the economic cost of justice; legal education and training; the manner in which legal procedures actually function; alternative dispute resolution methods; physical infrastructure; public perception of the administration of justice; and the impact of judicial decisions on society. Regardless of the range of problems identified, though, he asserted that reform projects must begin, for the reasons he noted earlier, by focusing on the role of the judge.

The Bank aims to develop a "critical mass" of judges — perhaps ten percent of the judiciary — committed to and willing to lead reform efforts from within the judiciary itself. This critical mass is viewed as the key to changing the judicial culture from subservience or indifference to political and economic influence to independence and autonomy in fairly and fully applying the legal norms of a society. Once reform takes root within the judiciary, reform initiatives can expand to include other judicial system actors and contemplate necessary constitutional or legislative changes -- now that it is likely that the judges will enforce those efforts to institutionalize judicial independence.

Mr. MacLean stated that the Bank's approach could be summed up in three words: service, leadership and participation. In all of the Bank's projects participation is featured early in the development process. Initially, that includes interviews and consultations with relevant governmental and non-governmental entities (judges, government officials, bar associations, trade associations, law schools, chambers of commerce and NGOs). He maintained that participation has been and will continue to be part of the Venezuela judicial reform project.

Finally, Mr. MacLean cautioned that the World Bank is limited by its charter to focusing on activities that are "economic" in nature, ruling out assistance in the areas of prison reform and criminal law, for example. He insisted, though, that reforms targeted to assist economic development also address many of the social and economic rights of citizens. He also stated that no contradiction exists between the Bank's initial focus on administrative reforms and the need to attack corruption because an efficient and transparent judicial administration can do much to identify and reduce the kind of unbridled judicial discretion and lack of management control that permit economic and political influence to permeate the judiciary.

The Inter-American Development Bank. Ms. Biebesheimer noted that the IDB's role in judicial reform grew out of a conference on judicial reform in Costa Rica in 1993, and a decision by the Bank's Board of Governors in 1994 to focus resources on poverty reduction and social equity;

environmental protection; and the modernization of the state and strengthening of civil society. The Bank's mandate in this new area is to promote strengthening and modernization of the judicial system.

Within the area of justice reform, Bank activities may include i) modernization of the legal framework and the promotion of basic citizen rights; ii) the administrative strengthening of the judicial branch; iii) the establishment of alternative dispute resolution methods; iv) the execution of programs of legal aid and legal education for the population; v) human resources development; and vi) increasing public safety.

Ms. Biebesheimer outlined four broad strategies for IDB work in this area: IDB projects should grow out of a comprehensive reform strategy developed by the state; a broad political consensus (including civil society) on the need for and scope of reform is essential for long-term success; projects need not be large — a series of modest reform initiatives may be appropriate in some states; and the bank's work should focus on building a local capacity to continue reform efforts. The IDB's first judicial reform initiatives are focused in Central America — Costa Rica received the first bank assistance in this area in 1995. Projects were approved for Honduras and El Salvador in March 1996. She noted that while the IDB's focus is economic and social development, it has also moved into new areas, even including criminal justice issues, where improvements are seen as necessary to enable development to occur. The IDB's charter does not restrict or prohibit its focus on these issues.

Venezuelan Judiciary Perspective. Magistrate Gisela Parra, a member of the Judicial Council, the government body charged with implementing the World Bank-supported Venezuela Infrastructure Project, focused her remarks on the Project. She noted that the effort to improve Venezuela's judicial system has been both challenging and difficult, so much so that without the intervention of the World Bank, it is doubtful that Venezuela would have undertaken the reform effort. The Project has enabled a process of structural reform by the incorporation of information technology and of education and specialized training for judges to instill leadership capacity. In her view, the low profile of the project contributed to its early survival; broader participation might have attracted opposition from important elements which would have doomed the possibility for any progress at all.

Ms. Parra believes that judicial reform must focus on the user of the system, the person who needs to have his or her disputes settled. Judges have seen themselves as the owners of their court, sometimes even separate from civil society; focus on the judicial mentality is therefore indispensable. A remaining challenge is to involve civil society. NGOs have an important role to play, but must be more constructive. The reform process must go beyond technical aspects, but in deciding on next steps, it must be Venezuelans who determine the framework of reform. A national and political consensus is necessary for the success of reform initiatives. Technical support from the World Bank has been important in reaching this point.

NGO Perspective. Ms. Ligia Bolívar, who directs Provea's Legal and Judicial Reform Project, highlighted key concerns about the Venezuela Project. She began by noting that since Provea's creation in 1988, it has focused attention in two areas: i) criticism of lack of access to justice and the lack of an autonomous Judicial Council; and ii) calling for an independent judiciary, including the need for institutional strengthening, and developing the judicial career; budgetary improvements; and improvements in the administration of the courts.

She criticized the Project's narrow focus and the reluctance to address the fundamental problem of judicial independence from a structural point of view; the Bank's restricted definition of judiciary "consumers"; the failure to involve the wider governmental and non-governmental community in the project development process (a deficiency she notes is now being addressed, but must go further).

Ms. Bolívar also stated that there is a false dichotomy between what is "economic" or "non-economic" in judicial and legal reform efforts. The objective should be to create a good and fair justice system in which the same rules apply to everyone. Economic development can be hindered, for instance, when land rights of peasants are ignored; similarly, economic disruption can occur when conflict develops as a result of failure to protect labor or worker rights. The conception of development must not exclude these issues.

Ms. Bolívar then addressed the issue of the appropriate role for multilateral development banks in judicial reform activities. The fundamental question is the extent to which the intervention of MDBs is appropriate. Provea is opposed to conditionality, but it is also against a neutral vision of reform which is divorced from reality. The World Bank must not provide a "blank check," but must take steps to ensure that government commitments are being fulfilled. As to the appropriate role of NGOs, Ms. Bolívar said while NGOs should not replace the state, they have an important contribution to make, which can take a variety of forms, from the identification of needs, to project implementation, to project evaluation. She concluded by saying that when Provea undertook the Project with the Lawyers Committee to examine the Venezuela loan, they viewed the project with skepticism. Now they are cautiously optimistic.

Comments from participants. NGO participants offered their views on the banks' approaches to judicial reform. The comments, however, focused almost exclusively on the role of the World Bank, given its recent involvement in the development of reform initiatives in Argentina, Ecuador, Bolivia and Peru subsequent to the launch of the Venezuela project, and the limited work of the IDB in the area to date. Comments largely drew upon Mr. MacLean's statements, a draft of the report on the World Bank in Venezuela which had been circulated prior to the meeting, and the experiences of NGO participants from countries where the World Bank is — or has been — involved in reform discussions or projects.

NGO participants questioned what a number referred to as the Bank's "narrow scope" in its reform projects, particularly its reluctance to insist on the need for a long-term comprehensive plan. Mr. MacLean rejected the characterization of the Bank's vision as "narrow," and insisted that the Bank recognizes that (i) securing judicial independence and autonomy are critical to the fashioning of a judiciary that can defend the rule of law and (ii) a comprehensive plan is essential to the long-term success of reform. NGO participants maintained that, in practice, reform projects turned out to be more limited than Bank statements and publications suggest.

NGO participants raised these concerns when contesting Mr. MacLean's assertion that judicial reform efforts should focus initially to such a degree on the judge. While agreeing that efforts to change the judicial culture should play a prominent role in any reform effort, participants disagreed with the claim that structural changes would be fruitless until the judicial culture has been modified. NGO arguments covered several broad areas:

- Although Mr. MacLean insisted otherwise, the judge-focused approach tends in fact to mitigate against the development of a long-term, comprehensive reform plan supported by a broad political consensus prior to the initiation of any reform efforts. This reform strategy suggests years of quietly working with judicial administration, court management and judge development and training before opening up the process to broad scrutiny and discussion. This approach contradicts the Bank's own insistence on the necessity for broad-based reform involving the entire judiciary, the government, the legal community and relevant representatives of civil society. It also leads, in the view of many, to piecemeal, uncoordinated reform projects that lack broad political support. Venezuelan participants pointed to their experience as an example of the problems that ensue from a reform approach that quietly focuses on only one part of the judicial system (the initial World Bank plan addressed only strengthening the ability of the Judicial Council to manage courts). Its scope expanded to include the judges themselves as work on the ground revealed the sorry state of judicial capacity. But most of the judiciary entities were not involved and had no idea what was going on; no broad government support was ever obtained; and no strategy for follow-on reform was developed.
- The political manipulation of justice systems and endemic corruption were cited by all participants as the most pressing problems in the area of judicial reform. Again, Mr. MacLean insisted that these are primary Bank concerns as well, but that the only way to achieve them in the long run is to create a group of judges that will defend the independence of judicial institutions and weed out corrupt colleagues.

However, several participants argued that even the development of a core of good judges can be defeated by the constitutional ability of a president or congress to remove judges at will or at the end of short terms, or to expand the size of courts to dilute their influence. Thus, constitutional and other legal changes to protect the independence of judges (*e.g.*, life terms with no reduction in benefits) may be necessary to protect judges from political attack.

- NGO participants also pointed out that the development of a core of outstanding, reform-minded judges has its limitations — most judges will be, at best, of ordinary moral character and legal ability and will need strong institutional support and oversight to resist political and economic influence. This institutional support might come from three directions — establishing judicial selection procedures that reduce the role of political factors and emphasize legal experience and a reputation for fairness and impartiality, legally strengthening the independence of the entity administering the courts, and/or creating a widely-respected judicial disciplinary panel with powers to sanction and dismiss judges. These initiatives usually require constitutional and/or legislative changes.
- NGO participants also noted that efforts to create a functioning justice system can also be thwarted by bad laws — the establishment of "faceless" (secret) courts, for example, to try those accused of terrorist or political violence. Another example concerned the ability of the executive and/or congress to manipulate jurisdiction to give military courts the right to hear certain classes of crimes. Impunity followed political interference and corruption as major concerns, and impunity is fostered by the removal of jurisdiction over police and military crimes from civilian courts. Constitutional and/or code changes may be necessary to keep crimes classified as human rights violations in the hands of excellent civilian judges.

In addition, many NGOs noted the need for constitutional or legislative change to provide standing to sue for groups or individuals to represent the public at large in the defense of public rights (e.g., to stop environmental pollution). Overly restrictive standing requirements, the need to show individual injury, no class-action option, and no mechanism for court-or- losing party absorption of costs were cited as barriers that block effective realization of many economic, social, cultural, civil and political rights.

- Finally, a number of NGO participants found the notion of focusing on the character of judges vague. They argued that the Bank may have no real idea how change in a judicial "culture" comes about, nor how changes in the "character" (another slippery concept) of a small group of judges can transform the nature of a judicial system.

On access to justice issues, participants were equally concerned. While the World Bank has tended to focus broadly on access as a function of the fairness and efficiency of the courts (*e.g.*, not even wealthy corporations would want to use unreliable courts), Mr. MacLean also acknowledged the importance of access for the poor and cited examples of small farmers in Peru and indigenous peoples in Ecuador who lack effective access to courts. NGO participants focused on barriers to the use of the courts by the 70% or more of the Latin American population in poverty. Land disputes, labor disputes, family disputes and the need to defend constitutionally-guaranteed social, health, education and environmental rights leave the poor in greater need than the wealthy for access to justice. And while Mr. MacLean noted the fact that the lawyer's monopoly on legal representation increased access-to-justice problems, it was pointed out that constitutional and/or legislative changes would be needed to address this issue as well. Participants insisted that a justice system exists for the benefit of all of a society's members, not just those who seek to resolve economic disputes of a traditional nature. Any reform initiative must include the access issue among its top concerns.

The access to justice issue lead to another concern — the definition of the "users" or "consumers" of a judicial system. While the World Bank's strategy seemed to focus on commercial actors, participants insisted that reform measures must apply to every social actor interested in vindicating economic, social, cultural, civil and political rights in the courts. Participants expressed dismay at the possibility that reform efforts focused on narrow economic sectors could create two judicial classes, one commercial, with access to an efficient court system, the other, with non-commercial claims, condemned to deal with a debilitated judiciary. It was argued that certain rights and environmental protections should be a priority area for legal reform since the state's monopoly over such matters effectively precludes recourse outside the traditional justice system.

B. Participation in Project Development and Implementation

The second day of the conference focused on the process of project development and opened with a discussion of the role of non-governmental actors in contributing to the development and implementation of judicial reform initiatives. Both banks have formal participation policies, and both representatives addressed the question.

The Inter-American Development Bank. Ms. Biebesheimer stated that the IDB is committed to broad consultation with and the participation of civil society organizations in all of its modernization of the state projects, including judicial reform. She said the bank seeks out and encourages governments to involve civil society institutions, including human rights and environmental NGOs, in the design of projects, since broad-based participation is viewed as essential to identify local needs and to obtain the political consensus necessary for the long-term success of reform. In fact, she noted, consensus-building may be a IDB-funded project in and of itself. She referred to the Costa Rica judicial reform project as an example — the project development process was highly participatory, with public meetings held all over the country. In Honduras, the IDB is supporting seminars at which the issues of constitutional reform before the Congress can be discussed and debated. This kind of participation has an additional benefit in that it may help the bank identify organizations that can provide development and social services locally with technical assistance and training.

The World Bank. Mr. MacLean argued that broad participation must occur at the proper moment in the development of a project. He reiterated that the World Bank strives to consult a broad range of economic "consumers" of judicial reform during its early work investigating country conditions and needs and in project design. He emphasized that broad public participation should usually occur after commitment to reform has been secured within the judiciary itself. Only then would civil society have a reform plan to critique and the judges, buttressed by a "core" reform group, be comfortable with public scrutiny of the judicial system. At that point, civil society can be mobilized to carry reform forward, pursuing the legislative and constitutional changes that may be necessary to secure the independence of the court system. Venezuela, he noted, was now reaching the point where broad participation would be welcome, after nearly two years of working to convince the judges of the necessity for reform.

NGO Perspective. Once again, few of the participants had direct experience with the IDB's recent ventures into judicial reform. Most of the comments were therefore directed at the World Bank's participation policies and record. Ms. Patricia Armstrong, coordinator of the International Financial Institutions Program of the Lawyers Committee for Human Rights, described both the World Bank's general participation policy as reflected in Bank documents and the emphasis on the importance of broad participation in legal reform contained in a "lessons learned" paper produced by the Bank's legal department. She also pointed out the importance of the timing of participation in relation to the banks' "project cycle" — the formal phases a project must pass through from the time informal discussions begin between a country and the Bank and the time the Board approves financing and implementation of the project actually begins. The most effective (and also most difficult) points of intervention are early in the process — the project identification, preparation and staff appraisal stages prior to the point where Executive Director approval drastically reduces the opportunity for modifications.

Comments from participants. NGO participants were uniformly critical of the World Bank's approach to participation, noting that participation after a project has already been designed and partially implemented leaves no room for the most important reason for broad consultations — an accurate assessment of local needs from all the users of the judicial system. Few shared the concern (highlighted with an example from Bank work in Argentina) that open meetings would result in unfocused discussions unable to produce a consensus proposal and judges unwilling to comment on their work in public. It was noted that broad consultative efforts take time and can generate a vast amount of (often contradictory) analyses of judiciary problems and ideas for solutions, but that the purpose of such discussions is to ensure that all concerns are heard, and different options and proposals considered seriously. Bank and government technicians should then be able to design a long-range strategy and discrete projects fully aware of the needs and concerns of both the legal system and society at large. Some NGO participants noted that broad consultations can help to focus public debate on the legal system and serve as a key, first step in generating broad public support for reform.

NGO participants generally were more concerned about another Bank example in Argentina — Bank officials being "captured" by an executive (or a small judiciary leadership) interested in maintaining control over the courts and discouraged from consulting with legal scholars, institutes or NGOs with views of the problems of the legal system different from those of the government. And in Venezuela, it was pointed out, the design of the judicial reform project was based on consultations with a very small group of judges, lawyers and private commercial organizations. Once again, many participants noted, the gap between World Bank policy encouraging broad participation and the way, in fact, this policy is implemented on the ground is very wide.

NGO participants maintained that NGOs can play a highly positive role in the design and implementation of legal and judicial reform projects if the banks would take their views into account. Legally-oriented NGOs, whether concerned about the environment, human rights or other issues, tend to be the "consumers" *par excellence* of judicial systems who can offer a valuable perspective of a judiciary's problems, which in many cases may be dramatically different from that of the government, investors or commercial entities. They utilize the judicial system to enforce fundamental rights — and have no alternative way of vindicating the interests of their clients. Thus, their stake in successful judicial reform is enormous. But, all insisted, participation must be broad-based (including all interested groups and individuals), timely (early in the project design phase) and meaningful (not *pro forma* or solely informational).

C. Conclusions

The conference represented the first group meeting of legally-oriented human rights and environmental NGOs and representatives of the World Bank and IDB to discuss judicial reform in Latin America. The fact that both banks sent representatives to exchange perspectives with 21 NGOs from the region was itself viewed as a highly positive and encouraging first step toward greater communication between the banks and NGOs in this area.

Although Mr. MacLean insisted throughout that the World Bank and the NGO participants shared the same goal — helping states to develop independent, honest and efficient judicial systems — the conference did point out several important differences in strategy. First, NGO participants insisted that reform projects should be designed at the outset with the broad participation of governmental, legal and non-governmental actors to best identify local needs and priorities build support for long-run changes. While Mr. MacLean agreed that broad consultation was necessary during initial needs assessment stages of project planning, he also indicated that broad participation should take place only after the judicial structure for reform is in place. The differences are those of timing, sequence and emphasis.

Second, participants felt that reform proposals should be comprehensive, integrating all judicial actors with a series of different projects phasing in over several years. While the World Bank would agree in principle with this view, in practice some Bank-funded projects have narrowly focused on one judicial actor and have been carried out in the absence of any long-run government strategy.

Third, it was felt critically important that the government clearly commit to reform from the outset, demonstrating that commitment with constitutional and/or legislative changes designed to improve the selection and oversight of judges and give the judicial sector greater institutional independence from the executive and political parties. Mr. MacLean was clearly less sanguine about the usefulness of such measures prior to the development of a core of judges committed to carrying out reform. And, perhaps in a reflection of that view, it was pointed out that few, if any, governments have been called upon to examine structural impediments to judicial independence and autonomy in Bank-funded projects and few have. And, again, while the Bank identifies government ownership and commitment to long-term reform as important, these policies do not always translate into practice on the ground.

Fourth, participants felt it crucial that governments establish a mechanism for coordinating reform projects sponsored by different development aid organizations, both multilateral and bilateral. Again, Mr. MacLean agreed with this point, noting the initial failure to do so in Venezuela as a lesson for future projects.

Finally, the participants and the bank representatives did agree that the exchanges of information and views had been highly informative and useful. Both Mr. MacLean and Ms. Biebesheimer made themselves available in Washington to any of the participants or other NGOs who wished to discuss these issues and noted that the each of their institutions was in an ongoing process of learning from each of its reform experiences. The NGO participants agreed to form a network to exchange information on judicial and legal reform initiatives throughout Latin America and to share strategies for working with the banks, governments and other organizations active in the area of judicial reform.

CONFERENCE PARTICIPANTS

Non-Governmental Organizations:

ARGENTINA
Centro de Estudios Legales y Sociales (CELS)
Emilio F. Mignone, President

Fundación Ambiente y Recursos Naturales (FARN)
Dr. Daniel Alberto Sabsay
Director of International Relations

BOLIVIA
Asamblea Permanente de los Derechos Humanos de Bolivia
Dr. Waldo Albarracín Sánchez, President

BRAZIL
Instituto Apoio Jurídico Popular (AJUP)
T. Miguel Pressburger, Coordinator

Instituto Socioambiental
Carlos Frederico Marés de Souza Filho, President

CHILE
Facultad de Derecho, Departamento de Investigación y Extensión
Universidad Diego Portales
Prof. Jorge Correa Sutil

COLOMBIA
Comisión Colombiana de Juristas
Gustavo Gallón Giraldo, Director

Equipo ILSA
Germán Burgos

Fundación para la Defensa del Interés Público (FUNDEPUBLICO)
Claudia Mora

Appendix A

COSTA RICA
Centro de Derecho Ambiental y de los Recursos Naturales
Lizbeth Espinoza Espinoza

ECUADOR
Corporación Latinoamericana para el Desarrollo (CLD)
Valeria Merino Dirani, Executive Director

Corporación ESTADE
Ramiro Montalvo, Program Director

MEXICO
Centro de Derechos Humanos "Miguel Agustín Pro Juárez"
David Fernández Dávalos, Director
(for Red Nacional de Organizaciones Civiles de Derechos Humanos "Todos los Derechos para Todos")

Centro Mexicano de Derecho Ambiental
María Elena Mesta Fernández

PERU
Centro de Estudios y Acción para la Paz
Roger Niego Arana
(for Coordinadora Nacional de Derechos Humanos)

Sociedad Peruana de Derecho Ambiental
Carlos Chirinos Arrieta

Comisión Andina de Juristas
Samuel Bernardo Abad Yupanqui

UNITED STATES
Lawyers Committee for Human Rights
Robert Weiner, Coordinator, Americas Program
Patricia Armstrong, Coordinator, IFI Program
Patrick J. Gavigan, Consultant

VENEZUELA
Programa Venezolano de Educación-Acción en Derechos Humanos (Provea)
Ligia Bolivar

Red de Apoyo por la Justicia y la Paz
Laura Roldan

Oficina de Derechos Humanos, Vicariato Apostolico
Luis Jesús Bello

FUJUCAVI
Mariolga Quintero Tirado

Multilateral Development Banks:

WORLD BANK
Roberto G. MacLean
Legal Reform and Advisory Services
Legal Department

INTER-AMERICAN DEVELOPMENT BANK
Christina Biebesheimer
State and Civil Society Unit

Venezuelan Government:

Judicial Council (Consejo de la Judicatura)
Gisela Parra

Comisión Presidencial para la Reforma del Estado (COPRE)
Julio César Fernández Toro, Executive Secretary
Jose Miguel Torreaba

Judiciary School (Escuela de la Judicatura)
Ximena Rodriguez de Canestri

Ministry of Justice (Ministerio de Justicia)
José Armando Mejias

APPENDIX B

The World Bank
INTERNATIONAL BANK FOR RECONSTRUCTION AND DEVELOPMENT
INTERNATIONAL DEVELOPMENT ASSOCIATION

1818 H Street N.W.
Washington, D.C. 20433
U.S.A.

(202) 477-1234
Cable Address: INTBAFRAD
Cable Address: INDEVAS

July 11, 1996

Ms. Patricia Armstrong
International Financial Institutions Program
Lawyers Committee for Human Rights
330 Seventh Avenue, 10th Floor
New York, NY 10001

Dear Tish:

Thank you for your letter of July 5 concerning the draft Venezuela report and for the opportunity to provide comments. It is regrettable that the Spanish language version was finalized by Provea without our input and circulated at the Caracas meeting. As you know, we were advised that the report would not be finalized prior to receipt of our comments after the meeting. I hope that you will be able to pass on the comments in this letter to Provea so that they can make the appropriate corrections in any subsequent printing.

First of all, even though the paper is described as a case study of the Venezuela Project, there are a number of general statements in the paper regarding the Bank's approach to judicial reform not only in Venezuela but also in other countries. The tone and detail of many of these statements is quite misleading.

At the outset, it is important to reiterate that the principal mandate of the Bank is to promote economic development in its member countries. The Bank is prohibited by its Articles of Agreement from being influenced by the "political character" of its member countries, from interfering in the political affairs of any member, and from allowing political factors or events to influence its decisions. Political considerations are therefore irrelevant to the Bank's work unless it is established that they have direct and obvious economic effects relevant to the Bank's work, in which case those economic effects may be taken into account. The authors of the paper appear to feel that this position is the result of a narrow and arguable interpretation of the Articles (pp. 10-11). However these limitations were explicitly and carefully crafted by the founders of the Bank and from the outset have been accepted by the Bank's shareholders and management as necessary to prevent the work of the Bank from becoming politicized. The difficulty of deciding where the dividing lines lie in some specific circumstances (noted at page 11) does not detract from the clarity of the general principle expressed in the Articles.

RCA 248423. ⊔ WUI 64145 ⊔ FAX (202) 477-6391

Ms. Patricia Armstrong -2- July 11, 1996

The paper describes (at page 12) the Bank's exclusion of political factors from its work as "technical", "functionalist" and "restrictive", and as a "narrow" reading of the Articles (page 58). In fairness to the readers of the paper, it should be noted by the authors that this policy is the result of a deliberate decision by the founders of the Bank in 1946, consistently adhered to over the years since the Bank's formation, and not simply a current interpretation placed on the Articles by the Bank's management.

The authors have also wrongly concluded that as a consequence of its exclusion of political factors from its work, the Bank is prevented from addressing fundamental issues of judicial reform such as independence of the judiciary. The Bank's view is that an effectively functioning judicial system is an important influence on the pace of economic reform in developing countries. There is no inconsistency then in the Bank addressing aspects of the judicial system which detract from the efficiency and fairness of the system and therefore from its effectiveness as a means of providing reliable dispute resolution services. It is very often the case that the same factors that contribute to a lack of judicial independence also lead to inefficiencies, reduced effectiveness and increased unreliability of the judicial process.

Accordingly the Bank can and does consider issues affecting the independence of the judiciary in the design of its judicial reform projects. As the paper notes at page 18, both the Ecuador and Peru judicial sector assessments include such issues as the appointment, removal and pay of judges, as well as recommendations of measures to improve the professionalism of the judiciary. As the Bank has noted in its recent publication "The Judicial Sector in Latin America and the Caribbean: Elements of Reform" (1996), judicial independence is more than simply freedom from political influence in individual cases. It includes structural, organizational and administrative aspects such as a transparent and merit-based appointment system, tenure which is either for life or subject to a transparent renewal system, the adoption of a code of judicial ethics to foster peer pressure for the maintenance of high standards of judicial conduct, judicial budgetary autonomy, and adequate and stable compensation packages for judges. The Bank's judicial reform projects aim to address these type of issues (indeed the paper notes at page 19 that the Russia Legal Reform Project includes components aimed at strengthening the independence of the judiciary), along with improvements in court management, case flow administration, ADR, and training for judges and court staff.

Perhaps because of the same misperception concerning the Bank's role, the paper argues (at page 2) that in its judicial reform work the Bank has ignored the need for long-term comprehensive sector reform strategies, and instead has concentrated on selected administrative reforms. While the Venezuela project in its initial design was narrowly focused, the Bank has worked with the Government over the last two years to progressively expand the sector linkages of the various components. The lessons of Venezuela have also been incorporated in our later work in Argentina, Ecuador, Peru and Trinidad & Tobago, where in each case a sector assessment was carried out with combinations of foreign and local consultants as well as Bank staff. And of course, these are Bank-financed projects carried out by governments and not by the Bank, so that project design is the result of a partnership between the Bank and the government concerned rather than a Bank product alone.

More generally, the Bank has continued to learn from its early experiences in the area of legal and judicial reform and to incorporate those lessons in its ongoing work. In addition to working with the Government of Venezuela to increase the sectoral focus of the Venezuela project, the Bank has broadened the scope of reforms covered in later projects in other countries, with the aim of achieving comprehensive sectoral and institutional change. The Russia Legal Reform Project is simply the most recent example of this approach.

At the same time, the Bank has sought to tap the opinions of affected groups in order to improve project design. Contrary to the various suggestions in the paper (for example, at pages 2 and 20) that the Bank is reluctant to involve judiciary and civil society organizations in the development of its judicial reform projects, the Bank has operationalized the goal of widespread consultation, both through meetings with interested groups and through workshops. Nonetheless, the extent of that consultation and the involvement of any particular NGO will inevitably vary depending upon the circumstances of the project concerned.

There are a couple of matters of detail I would like to draw to your attention. At page 19, there is a reference to the Russia Legal Reform Project. You might wish to say that the Project was approved by the Bank on June 13, 1996. On the same page, there is a list of other Bank legal reform projects under development or implementation. India and Poland should not be on the list. However, Georgia, Kazakhstan and Ukraine can be added.

We would be pleased to comment on a revised draft of the paper in due course.

Sincerely,

Douglas A. Webb
Legal Adviser
Legal Reform & Private Sector Development

LAWYERS COMMITTEE FOR HUMAN RIGHTS STAFF

PROVEA STAFF

RAÚL CUBAS, General Coordinator

Legal Defense
LIGIA BOLÍVAR
LORENA FERNÁNDEZ
MARIA ELENA RODRÍGUEZ
URSULA STRAKA

Human Rights Education
MARÍA ISABEL BERTONE, Coordinator
ENRIQUE GONZÁLEZ
ARMANDO GUERRA
ELBA MARTÍNEZ
SARA PÉREZ

Information and Documentation
ALVARO CABRERA, Coordinator
YBELICE BRICEÑO
FRANCISCO CASTILLO
ANTONIO GONZÁLEZ
URAIMA GUERRA
PAULA HERRERO
VICMAR MORILLO
GOIZEDER ODRIOZOLA

Administration
JANETH ANGULO
ARCÁNGELA ARNONE
JACQUELINE PEÑALOZA
OLGA VILLASMIL

Visiting Fellow
CALIXTO AVILA

The Venezuelan Program for Human Rights Education and Action (*Programa Venezolano de Educación - Acción en Derechos Humanos*: Provea), an independent organization based in Caracas, Venezuela, was founded in 1988 to protect and promote human rights through legal assistance and education. Its activities seek to uphold the standards guaranteed by the Universal Declaration of Human Rights and other national and international human rights laws and instruments ratified by Venezuela, especially in the field of economic, social and cultural rights. Provea's activities include human rights education at all levels, the preparation and dissemination of reports on human rights in Venezuela and the defense of human rights through legal and extra-judicial mechanisms available at national and international levels.

Provea
Apartado Postal 5156
Carmelitas 1010-A, Caracas, Venezuela
Tel. (58-2) 862-1011; Fax (58-2) 81-6669
E-mail: provea@conicit.ve

The Lawyers Committee for Human Rights was founded in 1978 and works to protect and promote fundamental human rights. Its work is impartial, holding each government to the standards affirmed in the International Bill of Human Rights. The Committee's Human Rights Program conducts fact-finding missions and publishes reports which serve as a starting point for follow-up work with locally-based human rights advocates and lawyers, with governments and with inter-governmental organizations such as the United Nations and the World Bank. The Committee's Refugee Project seeks to provide legal protection for refugees, including the right to dignified treatment and a permanent home.

Lawyers Committee for Human Rights
330 Seventh Avenue, 10th Floor
New York, NY 10001 USA
Tel. (212) 629-6170; Fax. (212) 967-0916
E-mail: comm@lchr.org

Washington, D.C. Office:
100 Maryland Avenue, NE
Suite 502
Washington, DC 20002 USA
Tel. (202) 547-5692; Fax. (202) 543-5999
E-mail: wdc@lchr.org